JEWISH CULTURE AND CUSTOMS
A Sampler of Jewish Life

BY STEVE HERZIG

JEWISH CULTURE AND CUSTOMS

A Sampler of Jewish Life

BY STEVE HERZIG

The Friends of Israel Gospel Ministry, Inc.
P. O. Box 908, Bellmawr, NJ 08099

JEWISH CULTURE AND CUSTOMS
A Sampler of Jewish Life

Copyright © 1997 by The Friends of Israel Gospel Ministry, Inc.
Bellmawr, New Jersey 08099

Herzig, Steve

Printed in the United States of America
Library of Congress Catalog Card Number: 97-075105
ISBN 0-915540-31-2

The Friends of Israel Gospel Ministry, Inc.
P. O. Box 908, Bellmawr, New Jersey 08099

Cover by Left Coast Design, Portland, OR
Artwork by Stan Stein of Stein Arts, Northfield, NJ

TABLE OF CONTENTS

DEDICATION

The sovereignty of God is illustrated no better than by His placing me into a Jewish home at birth. By His grace, I was given parents who made it very easy for me to understand a holy God. It is to them, Nathan and Blanche Herzig, that I dedicate this book. So much of the content of this volume is a glimpse into the life they provided for me.

INTRODUCTION

While visiting in the home of a Jewish family, I noticed the bulletin of the synagogue they attended. It listed a weekly meeting in which the rabbi would answer questions relating to Jewish culture and customs. Ignorance about their own beliefs and traditions has prompted the Jewish community to offer these helpful and popular classes.

If Jewish people are ignorant concerning some aspects of Jewish practice—and they are—imagine the lack of understanding that exists among the Gentile community. This void is of little concern to the majority of Gentiles, but there is one segment that does care a great deal. They are true Christians, born again and Bible-believing. They consider themselves people of God and have a tremendous love for the Jewish people. The reason for this is simple. Jesus the Messiah was born a Jew in Israel—the land God promised to His people. His followers were all Jews who practiced their faith. Anyone who holds the Scriptures to be the Word of God will desire a better understanding of the people He chose and called "the apple of his eye" (Zechariah 2:8).

Other books are available that provide explanations of Jewish practice and will be helpful to Jew and Gentile alike. Some of these books are listed in the back of this volume.

The book you hold in your hands was developed from the series entitled "Jewish Culture and Customs" featured in The Friends of Israel Gospel Ministry's well-known publication, *Israel My Glory*. Many favorable comments have been received regarding these articles, thanking the publisher for the clear, simple, and concise information. While we are grateful to be able to provide such information, this book has another objective. It is written with the hope that the reader will be able to link the many aspects of Judaism and the Jewish people to Christ and the Christian life.

This book does not exhaust the breadth and scope of the richness of Judaism or its people. As the Lord enables, it is my desire to follow this with another volume.

Now, please join me as we explore the world of Judaism and Jewish life.

MY TESTIMONY

LOX, BAGELS, AND THE BREAD OF LIFE

I was born in 1953 in Cleveland, Ohio, which has a Jewish population of about 80,000. I was raised in an Orthodox environment. I went to synagogue every Saturday, Hebrew school four days a week, Sunday school on Sunday, and Friday night service. Judaism was a seven-day-a-week affair for my family and me. I kept kosher and participated in many Jewish activities.

At the age of 18, while attending college, I met a born-again Christian. I didn't understand what the term *born again* meant, but over the next four years he and other Christians came into my life to explain such terminology and share spiritual truths with me. I, however, deeply resented that kind of presentation. I regarded this young man as a friend, but he was my adversary when it came to religious matters.

Before graduating from college, I went to California to visit my sister, and I learned that she was involved with a group called "The Friends of Israel Gospel Ministry." She shared the gospel with me, particularly the 53rd chapter of Isaiah. I immediately recognized that it was referring to Jesus, which was disturbing because of my background and family.

My sister invited me to attend a Friends of Israel Bible study. Quite frankly, the only reason I went was because they were serving free lox and bagels. She told me I didn't have to listen to the speaker or talk to anyone; all I had to do was go to the table, eat as much as I wanted, and wait until she was done (she was singing in a group that night). And that's exactly what I did. But I had to admit I was fascinated by the mix of people who attended the study—there were Jews, Gentiles, believers, and nonbelievers. They were nothing like my friends at college in Ohio, who were very radical and believed anything and everything. Rather, these were middle-aged people who had mortgages, car payments, and kids in school, and all—whether believers or not—told me they were searching for the truth. That was very interesting, and I went back to the table to take some literature, which, of course, was published by The Friends of Israel. That evening I went home, read the literature, and invited Jesus to come into my heart. But nothing happened. There was no explosion or vibration of the bed—my body didn't shake—so I thought God had rejected me.

A few days later, my sister and I went to Disneyland. While waiting in line to enter one of the attractions, I asked, "How do you know if you're born again?" She explained that people are born again when they understand that they are sinners and have received Jesus Christ into their hearts as their Savior from sin. I told her that I had done that but that I felt God had rejected me because I was still the same person. She then gave me my first lesson in discipleship. "Steve," she said, "God is going to make you the best *you* possible. Don't think that you're going to be just like us, because you're not. Take your eyes off of man and put them on the Lord Jesus."

Shortly thereafter, I moved to southern California, and for the next year a very godly man helped me to grow in Christ. He practiced his Bible study lessons as we played softball together, and, although he didn't realize it, he was instructing me in the Word of God. I attended his Bible study and went out on visitation with him. Later the leadership of The Friends of Israel extended an invitation to me to participate in their Atlantic City summer program, which I accepted. I spent the summer in Atlantic City and went on to Philadelphia College of Bible for two years of further Bible training.

I love the account of the blind man in John chapter 9. His response to the accusations concerning the person and work of Jesus was, "one thing I know, that, whereas I was blind, now I see" (John 9:25). I had the privilege of being born and raised in a wonderful Jewish family. They did the best they could to provide for me—at times sacrificially—the things I needed. Sovereignly, I was part of a people chosen by God. But, like the blind man, I could not see. I could not see that Jesus was the Messiah of Israel. But when my eyes were washed through His Word, I came away seeing.

In the providence of God, He chose me a second time. He chose me to be born again and placed me into a better family by providing the ultimate sacrifice—the death of the Son of God, the Messiah Jesus Christ. Like the blind man, I too can say, "one thing I know, that, whereas I was blind, now I see."

THE JEWISH PEOPLE

THE JEWS:
DIVERSITY WITH A COMMON LOYALTY

> The history of a people is like a river that flows
> between two banks. Even when it twists and
> winds through different lands, it is still the same
> river. It is the same river because its banks hold
> the waters together.[1]

"How can two people be so different and still be from the same family?" Haven't you heard this question asked? Children from the same parents, raised in the same home can look and act as if they are not even related.

So it can be with entire nations. The sons and daughters of Israel have a lineage that can be traced to Abraham, Isaac, and

Jacob. They have a land described as a place flowing with milk and honey. The Jewish people share a language of worship as rhythmic as music. They have a common loyalty grounded in a deep commitment to one God.

While it is true that Jewish people share many *family* traits, it is also true that they can be as different as night and day. All Jews do not look alike, nor do they all know Hebrew. They certainly do not all live in Israel. Their views on spiritual matters are as diverse as the colors of the rainbow.

This chapter examines the geographical and physical diversities within the Jewish race. The next chapter will examine their religious differences.

While the Assyrian and Babylonian captivities affected Jewish language and worship (some 30,000 Jews from the Middle East came to Israel speaking Aramaic), the harbinger of change came in 70 A.D. In absolute fulfillment of both the Old and New Testaments, the Temple was completely leveled, and God's Chosen People were scattered to the four corners of the earth. Two distinct groups emerged as the Jewish people began to settle: the Ashkenazic Jews and the Sephardic Jews. It has been said that the Sephardim were concerned with what they *should know*, while the Ashkenazim were concerned with what they *must do*.[2]

The Ashkenazim are traced to the northeast part of France and an area in Germany along the banks of the Rhine. Geography determined the kind of life these people lived and the language they spoke.

The medieval rabbis believed that the term *Ashkenaz* found in Jeremiah 51:27 refers to Germany.[3] Yiddish, the language that developed from this area, is a form of low German mixed with Hebrew and a number of other languages. It has been called the "Robin Hood" of languages, in that it steals from the linguistically rich to give to the poor.[4] It was the Yiddish language that bound together the millions of European Jews who immigrated to the United States at the turn of this century. Well before that oceanic exodus, however, there was the more gradual migration of these Jews into Poland, Austria-Hungary, and Russia.

The Ashkenazim "brought to eastern Europe a devotion to Talmudic studies in which they were to become the undisputed leaders."[5] This commitment *to do* caused them to isolate themselves from the world. They scorned the secular. Intellectual pursuit was limited to the Talmud and the Torah.[6] This same group of people was harassed and harangued through the Crusades, the pogroms, and the Holocaust. These Jews of eastern Europe were suppressed by the outside world, which saw them as Christ killers, devils, and subhumans.

A sect developed within the Ashkenazic Jews known as the Hasidim—the *pious ones*. They emphasized piety rather than learning, serving God through joy rather than denial. Their chief rabbi, the Tzaddik, is believed to be a miracle worker.[7] Israel b. Eliezer Ba'al Shem Tov, founder of modern Hasidism, summed up their philosophy by stating that all he had achieved had been through prayer, not study.

It was the Ashkenazic Jews who became peddlers, shoemakers, blacksmiths, and bakers. In the United States, most people equate *Yiddishkeit*, or *Jewishness*, with the Ashkenazic traditions. From them come *Fiddler on the Roof*, deli food, and such Yiddish expressions as "Oy vey!" and "chutzpah."

Distinctive both geographically and physically are the Jews who made their home in the Iberian Peninsula, which today is Spain and Portugal. They are known as the Sephardim, from the Hebrew word for Spain (Sepharad).

From the eighth century to the time of Columbus, these Jews enjoyed a golden age under the protection and encouragement of the Moors. The Moors (Muslims from North Africa) had a wonderful view of life as well as a love for the arts. In such an environment, the Sephardim were able to fulfill their desire *to know*.

The Jewish language that developed from this area of the world is known as Ladino. Like Yiddish, it is written in the Hebrew alphabet, but it is primarily Spanish peppered with Hebrew.

With the freedom allowed in this environment, the Jewish people became involved in their communities. The secular was not to be feared. They were drawn into learning, philosophy, medicine, law, and poetry.

The most revered Sephardic theologian was Moses, son of Maimon, also referred to as the Rambam—Rabbi Moses Ben Maimon. It is said of him, "From Moses to Moses, there is none like Moses."[8] Rambam gave the Jewish people the *Thirteen Principles of Faith*, one of which states, "I believe that the Messiah will someday come."

But the golden age did not last for the Spanish Jews. By the end of the 15th century, persecution was so great that they were forced to convert to Christianity or leave. In 1492 and 1497, Jews were expelled from Spain and Portugal. They began to settle in North Africa, Southern France, Italy, Turkey, Palestine, and the Balkans.[9] Many Jewish people in Spain were publicly baptized and became part of the church while continuing to practice their Judaism secretly by keeping kosher homes and observing the Sabbath. The Christians called them the *Marranos*, a Spanish word for *swine*. Among themselves they were called *Anusim—those who were forced*.[10]

The descendants of the Marranos were among the first Jews to settle in America. "Twenty-three men, women and children, aboard a French ship, the *St. Charles*, left for New Amsterdam, the Dutch colony that later developed into New York City, in the year 1654." [11]

The Sephardic rabbis developed their own system of rituals for the daily lives of their people. The *Shulchan Aruch*, or *prepared table*, covers laws of prayer, hygiene, and food. This code was not completely accepted by the Ashkenazic rabbis. Thus, today, differences still exist in customs and in some interpretations of the Law of Moses. Because of these differences, both Sephardic and Ashkenazic synagogues also exist.

Although the majority of Jewish people come from either Ashkenazic or Sephardic backgrounds, there are other, smaller groups of Jews in various parts of the world. In recent years, our attention has been focused on the Jews from Ethiopia. We have witnessed an historic event—truly a modern miracle—as almost an entire population of practicing Jews was flown from their geographical home in East Africa to their spiritual homeland in Israel. Although viewed by some as one of the "lost tribes," they are more probably the descendants of ancient converts to the God of Israel.

Since Israel became a state in 1948, Jewish people from all over the world have made *aliyah*; that is, they have returned to their national homeland. Their former homes—countries such as Yemen, Iran, Libya, Turkey, and Syria—are now almost completely free of Jews. Russian Jews by the hundreds of thousands, possibly as many as three million, are going to Israel. These Jews, who were raised in a Godless, Communist society, long to live in the land of their ancient forefathers. Russia, too, could be free of Jews by the end of this century. Recently, all the Jews in Albania left that country for a new home in Israel.

Not all Jews have left the places of their birth, however. India, South America, Mexico, Australia, New Zealand, South Africa, the United States, Canada, and parts of Europe maintain sizable Jewish populations. But the river of Judaism, although still divided, has begun to come together.

Yes, there is diversity within Judaism. Jewish people come in all sizes, shapes, and colors. They have lived or are living in just about every area of the world. Yet, within this diversity they have been bound together by one God and by the Book that He gave them. In the next section, we will see how they differ in interpreting that Book, the Bible, and how they approach the God who gave it to them.

DIFFERENT JEWS: THE VARIOUS BRANCHES OF JUDAISM

HEADLINE ISRAEL:
MESSIAH CAN'T BE FAR OFF...

Fundamentalist Jews are also interpreting the Gulf War as the catalyst that will hasten their own end-time scenario and their long-awaited Messiah.[12]

HEADLINE CHICAGO:
JEWS WHO DON'T BELIEVE IN GOD GATHER IN CHICAGO

What should Jewish people do who like bar mitzvahs, rabbis, Jewish weddings, Jewish holiday traditions, Bible stories and songs but do not believe in God? 1) Fake it? 2) Stay at home and sigh? 3) Join a temple with a congregation and a rabbi where no one believes in God?[13]

These headlines pose quite a contrast. It is important to note that these two groups are the extremes statistically. Only a small percentage of Jews hold either view.[14] But they do reflect just how difficult it is to explain what Jewish people believe.

Theology, as defined by Webster, is a "rational interpretation of religious faith, practice and experience." Christianity has been characterized by systematizing its theology. Books on systematic theology just do not exist in Judaism. Rather than developing a creed or system of belief, Judaism has defined itself more by its practices.

> [Judaism] has no dogma and lacks entirely any formal catechism which all believing Jews would accept....One must abandon absolutes in ritual and in dogma and examine instead the broad philosophy which underlies our faith. What we believe about the Bible, about miracles, about life after death, is secondary to what we believe about human potentialities and our responsibilities toward our fellow men.[15]

In ancient times, the Temple in Jerusalem was the common ground to which all Jews gathered to worship God according to His laws. Still, differences in interpretations of those laws made for diverse groups. We know of the Pharisees, Sadducees, Essenes, Zealots, and people of the land.[16] When the Temple was destroyed in 70 A.D. and the Jewish people scattered, interpretations of the Word of God became as widespread theologically as the people were geographically. Jews fled to the Far East, India, Ethiopia, Eastern Europe, and other countries along the Mediterranean. Cultural practices began to influence true biblical injunctions.

Volumes have been written to explain, define, or cate-
gorize the Jewish people and their beliefs. Let's examine the
most familiar branches of Judaism, the ones into which the
majority of the Jewish population fits today.

The Hasidim

No other branch of Judaism is more concerned with *doing*
than Hasidism (*the pious ones*). In all that he does, the Hasid is
to joy in God. Ba'al Shem Tov (Master of the Good Name),
founder of this movement, believed that there should be joy (*simcha*) in worship. All beliefs and practices are based on Proverbs
3:6, "In all thy ways acknowledge him."

Holiness is paramount to the Hasidic Jews. Being separate
and *fit* (*kosher*) for God are of utmost importance to them. A
wife is not fit or kosher to sleep with her husband during her
monthly cycle. Food is not kosher unless allowed by the Torah.
Clothing is not kosher unless modest. The list seems endless,
but the concept of being *fit* is essential to the understanding of
the Hasidim. They separate themselves physically from the rest
of the world as well.

The Hasidim live in many of the large cities of the world,
but they are best known in the Williamsburg and Crown
Heights sections of Brooklyn, New York, and in Mea-Shearim
in Jerusalem. These communities are patterned after the
shtetls (Jewish villages) of 18th-century Eastern Europe and
are completely self-sufficient. There is no need for any
exchange with outsiders; these *pious ones* keep to themselves
and their own kind.

Hasidic men wear long beards and dangling earlocks in
accordance with God's command in Leviticus 19:27, "Ye shall
not shave around your temples; neither shalt thou mar the cor-

ners of thy beard." They dress in exactly the same manner as their brethren did two hundred years ago: a wide-brimmed hat, black suit, white shirt buttoned at the neck, no necktie. The only exception to this dress is for special occasions such as the Sabbath, weddings, or high holidays, at which times they don great sable-trimmed hats called *shtreimels.*

The women dress more fashionably but always with extreme modesty. When a Hasidic woman marries, she cuts her hair (or even shaves her head) to show her modesty regarding her husband. Her head will always be covered, however, either with a wig or with a scarf of some kind.

The language spoken in Hasidic households—whether in the United States or Israel—is Yiddish. It is felt that Hebrew is too holy to be spoken and will be used only when the Messiah comes. Until that time, Hebrew is used only in the study of the holy books. The men most highly regarded in this ultra-Orthodox sect are their leaders, the *Tzaddiks.* This title comes from the Hebrew word meaning *righteous.* A Hasidic man was once asked who could replace his beloved "Rebbe" upon his death. The man answered, "We don't like to think about it. Only the Messiah Himself can replace so great a Tzaddik as the Rebbe."[17]

The Hasidim fervently believe in the coming of the Messiah. Their Messiah will not be a deity but, rather, a man empowered by God to bring peace to His people. Commitment to the law, both written and oral, performing *mitzvot* (*good deeds*), and assurance of an afterlife are basic beliefs of the Hasidim.

The Orthodox Tradition

Orthodox Jews share many common beliefs and practices with the Hasidim. They hold the *Halacha* (the *law*) in high

regard; they see the written and oral law as binding; they believe
that any problem facing them can be solved in the teaching of the
law; there is a strong emphasis on religious training for the children; the Sabbath is strictly observed; dietary laws are kept. And,
like the Hasidim, the Orthodox look for a powerful, personal
Messiah who will come to right the wrongs that have been per-
petrated over the years.

The major difference between the Orthodox and the
Hasidim is in their lifestyles. To these traditional Jews, commitment to their belief does not mean total separation from
the world. In what circumstances is a Jew defiled? To the
Orthodox, there is no defilement in wearing modern clothing,
provided that it is modest. Working outside the Jewish community is acceptable. The Rebbe is not the final authority.
Although the Orthodox have great respect for scholarship,
they are not as enthralled with the somewhat mystic elements
found in Hasidism. For the Orthodox Jew, there is no defilement in dependent thinking, as long as it remains within the
bounds of general tradition.

To use a phrase more familiar in Christian terminology,
Orthodox Jews feel they should be "*in* the world but not *of*
the world."

The Reform or Liberal Tradition ─────────

In his book *What the Jews Believe*, Rabbi Bernstein
alluded to the noted scientist Albert Einstein. He said,
"Although not observant of formal religion, [Einstein] is
profoundly Jewish in his religious outlook."[18] He quoted
Einstein as saying, "It is enough for me to contemplate the
mystery of conscious life perpetuating itself through all eter-
nity, to reflect upon the marvelous structure of the universe
which we dimly perceive...."[19]

If we are to understand the Reform Jew, we must understand two features of this quotation: first, the intellect of Einstein (Reform Jews value the intellect, the pursuit of knowledge to explain our world); and second, the statement "It is enough for me," which characterizes the independent, freethinking Jew. Reform Jews think and act independently of the written revelation of God because, for them, this revelation is, in fact, not from God but from mankind.

Reform Judaism "believes in progressive revelation and takes into account changes brought about through history."[20] Neither the Tenach (Bible) nor the Talmud (oral law) is binding. Men and women worship together, in colloquial language, complete with choir and organ.

Founded in 19th-century Germany, Reform Judaism is, for many Jews, the middle ground between assimilation and what they see as Jewish fanaticism. Because of the strong commitment to education and the emphasis on the intellectual, the Reform movement has encouraged, if not insisted upon, scientific logic to explain the world. Creation, miracles, and a personal Messiah are replaced with evolution, logic, and a messianic era brought about by mankind. Judaism that is true to the Torah looks for a future resurrection; Reform Judaism sees it as a time when mankind will awake to realize its potential. Torah-believing Jews practice their Judaism according to the Torah; Reform Jews are more interested in working out their Jewishness in a Gentile world.

The Conservative Tradition

Conservatism is the middle ground. Conservative Jews think in a way similar to Reform Jews, but they have a strong desire to maintain their *Yiddishkeit* (*Jewishness*) in worship and family life. In almost every aspect of Jewish life, the

Conservative lives a compromise between the Orthodox and Reform traditions. Worship in a Conservative synagogue is conducted half in Hebrew and half in colloquial language. Many Conservatives keep kosher at home but not necessarily in a restaurant or in someone else's home.

The goal of Conservative Jews is to carry on as much Jewish tradition as possible, maintain Jewish solidarity, and yet not have to fashion their lives around the beliefs and rituals of their more observant brothers.

Reconstructionism

"Both the idea and the movement owe their inspiration to Mordecai Menahem Kaplan."[21] For Kaplan, Judaism evolves. It is a system that must change with the culture in which it lives. In 1935 the magazine *Reconstructionist* was published using many of Kaplan's ideas. The concept of Jewish law was replaced with Jewish guidelines. A new prayer book was written, eliminating many traditional prayers and ideas. At the heart of this movement is not the person of God but, rather, the sociological reality of Judaism. The survival of the practice of being a Jew is very important. Jewish identity must be maintained, although achieving this is left to the individual, within very loose parameters.

Zionism

A word should be said about two other groups. The first is the Zionists. Zionism is not a branch of Judaism. People can be Zionists whether or not they are Jewish. Nor are all Jews Zionists. To be a Zionist, one must believe that the Jews have a right to a homeland called Israel situated in its ancient location. Hasidic Jews are not Zionists because they believe that Israel will be established as a nation only when the Messiah comes to establish His Kingdom there. Many Bible-believing Christians are Zionists because of their strong agreement with God's Word. God is a Zionist.

There are also those who do not concur with the Bible but who see Zionism as racist. The United Nations came to that conclusion some years ago. Still others see Zionism as some offbeat radical group.

Zionism was conceived by Theodor Herzl in 1897. It was born in 1948 with the founding and recognition of the State of Israel. It has since grown from infancy and childhood into its teen years, and it will come to full maturity when the Messiah Himself, the Lord Jesus, returns to the Mount of Olives to set up His Kingdom in His land.

Hebrew Christians

There remains yet another group of Jewish people who do not fit into the other existing branches of Judaism. These are the Hebrew Christians, also called completed Jews or Jewish believers. If people are born Jewish (that is, descendants of Abraham), they will die Jewish. Nothing can change that. What they believe may, however, change. Any person who receives Jesus as his or her Messiah becomes a new creation in his or her heart. Believing Jews can never go back to what they were, nor should they want to. In Christ, they have become a part of a body, a family of fellow believers whose head is Christ Himself.

Each of the groups we have looked at is sincere in its own beliefs and practices. Each of the traditional branches of Judaism tries to reach and/or please God in its own ways, most of which are inconsistent with the Word that God Himself gave to them. But the greatest Jew who ever lived did something none of us could ever do. He fulfilled the law and became the perfect sacrifice for the evil brought into this world. Jewish Christians have the best of both worlds: the rich heritage, "the glory, and the covenants, and the giving of the law, and...the promises" (Romans 9:4), and the fulfillment of those promises, the Messiah Himself, Jesus our Lord.

A JEW? OR NOT A JEW?

A rabbi tells a story of his days in rabbinical school. As part of his curriculum, the professor asked his students to list the names of the ten greatest Jews of the 20th century. The students wrote such names as Einstein, Freud, and Herzl. Upon completing their lists, the professor asked them to name the synagogue each of these great Jews attended. In most cases, the students could not place synagogues with the people they had listed. Yet, in the minds of the students, there was no question of the Jewishness of the people they had named. The point being made was that practice had little to do with identity. According to the professor, Jewishness should be determined by devotion to the Jewish people and the community, not by practice.

A young Jewish boy conducted his own survey—nothing official and by no means scientific. It was merely a point of interest to him, but his standards were high as he quizzed his friends. "Did you eat anything before coming to synagogue?" He then posed the question to other Jewish young men as they took their seats in the synagogue. The time and setting were of utmost importance—it was Yom Kippur, the Day of Atonement, regarded by many Jewish people as the most holy day of the year. When his friends answered positively, the young boy immediately pronounced the harshest of judgments: "Goy!" (Gentile). In that young man's mind, breaking the command to fast on that day disqualified a person from being a Jew.

In 1968, the Israeli Ministry of Interior refused to identify Lieutenant Commander Benjamin Shalit's two children as Jewish because their mother was a Gentile. Shalit argued that the government of Israel had no right to use religion in judging nationality. He felt that religious observance is not part of the concept of Jewishness. After much debate and argument, the Israeli Supreme Court ruled in his favor. That decision lasted for only one day because of incredible opposition by one of the prominent although small religious political parties. The party threatened to topple the government by pulling out of the ruling coalition in the government unless the court reversed itself. It did.

The question of Jewish identity is a hotly contested topic. It is a virtual tug-of-war involving Jewish theologians, rabbis, lawyers, judges, and government officials. Is a person Jewish because he or she identifies with a Jewish community? Is a person a Jew because he or she follows a certain code of behavior or practice? Can a Jew still be a Jew and live outside of Israel? Does it matter what he or she believes or does to be classified as a Jew? What about children born into a home where one parent is Jewish and the other is Gentile? So, who is a Jew? Is it a religion or a race? Is it a nationality or an ethnicity?

If Judaism is defined by practice, the question must be asked, Whose practice? Consider that the structure of Judaism has seldom been stagnant. Today, for instance, there are no animal sacrifices, which means no priestly functions. The reason is, of course, that the Temple has been but a memory since its destruction in 70 A.D. In addition, the Pharisees, Sadducees, Essenes, and Zealots have been replaced by the Hasidim, Orthodox, Conservative, Reform, and Reconstructionists. Each group differs in practice, yet each strongly believes itself to be Jewish. Also, consider that intermarriage is at an all-time high, resulting in scores of children who identify with the Jewish people. In which category should they be placed?

Today Israel recognizes only the Orthodox view as binding. The views of the other groups are deemed illegitimate. The Orthodox view states that if the mother is Jewish, the children will be Jewish. If the mother is a Gentile, the children are regarded as Gentiles. There are two reasons for this position. First, the mother has a tremendous impact on her children, presumably because she spends the bulk of family time with them. Second, we can be absolutely certain of the maternity of a child but not as certain of the paternity. Thus, the child of a Gentile mother who resides in Israel, serves in the Israeli army, and lives in an atmosphere of Jewishness, is not considered Jewish. However, a child of two Jewish parents who has no desire to participate in or practice Judaism, who might not even believe in God, is considered Jewish.

Also considered part of the identity debate are the several thousand people who have two Jewish parents but have committed themselves to follow the Jew from Nazareth—Jesus—whom they know to be the Messiah of Israel. According to rabbinic law, they are still Jews—albeit *meshumed* (*traitors*). According to the Israeli Supreme Court, however, Jews forfeit their "right of return" to the land of Israel as citizens if they make known their belief in Jesus. This position has been challenged in Israeli court on more than one occasion, but each time the ruling has been against the believer.

The biblical standard seems to agree with the rabbis and contradict the Israeli Supreme Court. First, being a Jew is a matter of blood. In light of the Holocaust, that statement may frighten some people. But a thorough understanding of the Abrahamic Covenant makes it clear that all people who are descendants of Abraham,

Isaac, and Jacob are Jewish. In the Jewish Scriptures there are numerous examples of disobedient Jews. That truth does not annul the fact that they are still Jews. That logic should follow that practice—or even lack of it—does not remove Jewishness.

Further, when a child is born into a mixed marriage, that child should be considered Jewish. There is biblical precedent with David, who is generally recognized as Israel's greatest Jewish king. He had two Gentile women in his genealogy: Ruth, his great-grandmother, and Rahab, his grandmother.

To be a Jew is a good thing. To be a believing Jew is the best. The first brings an identification to the Chosen People of God. The second brings a person to the eternal place of God.

HILLEL: THE KIND PHARISEE

Jewish tradition states that the oral law was transmitted from Moses to Joshua, from Joshua to the elders, from the elders to the prophets, and from the prophets to the men of the great assembly (*Knesseth Ha-Gadolah*). The members of the great assembly, called *Soferim*, or scribes, were believed to have originated with Ezra and Nehemiah after the Babylonian Captivity. The identities of many of the scribes are unknown, but they left a legacy to "be deliberate in judgment, raise up many disciples, and build a fence around the law." The "fence" would insure that the laws of God would not be broken because the laws of religious men would be placed "in front" of them. After several centuries, the *Sanhedrin* (consisting of 71 members) emerged and continued the unbroken line back to Moses.

The leaders of the Sanhedrin were the *Rosh* or *Nasi* (*president*) and the *Ab Beth Din* (*Father of the House of Judgment*). Together they were called *Zugoth* or *pairs* of teachers. They passed two laws that influence Judaism to this day. The first was compulsory provision for the education of children with no fathers, and the second was that there be a school in every community with at least ten families. These laws would guarantee that young Jewish boys would grow up knowing their prayers and Torah. "Torah Tzivah Lanu Moshe Morasha Kehilat Ya'akov"—The Torah which Moses taught us is the inheritance of the Jewish people.

The rule of the Sanhedrin by the Zugoth lasted for five generations. The most famous of these great teachers was Hillel. Referred to as the "elder" (*Zaken*) or the "Babylonian," he served as the last Rosh of the Sanhedrin from 30 B.C. to 10 A.D. These years were strategic in Israel's religious history. Herod was ruling in Jerusalem, the Pharisees and Sadducees had begun to develop gaping rivalries, the priesthood was deteriorating, and Messianic hopes were high. Hillel's rise to leadership came as a result of three notable characteristics: his love for the Torah, his love for wisdom, and his love for mankind. Stories about Hillel abound, and they usually highlight one of these characteristics.

At the age of 40, Hillel left Babylon to pursue studies in Israel, in the school of Sehmaya and Abtalyon. Unable to pay the admission fee to the academy, tradition asserts that he climbed to the roof to a skylight, where he could hear the lectures of the great teachers. Deeply engrossed in a lecture, the young scholar did not notice that heavy snow had begun to fall. When the teachers looked up to see the snow through the skylight, they saw the shadow of a man. The snow had completely covered him, but his love of learning was so intense that he never noticed. Hillel pursued any field of study that would help him to magnify and exalt the Torah. He became so highly regarded that it was said of him, "He was worthy of having the Sabbath profaned on his behalf." It is even said that he personally instructed Jesus of Nazareth.

Hillel made two notable contributions to Judaism. He was the creator of the *tannaim* (*rabbis*). The tannaim interpreted the Torah for the next 210 years, until the completion of the Mishna. He also divided the oral law into six divisions that provided the framework for the tannaim to complete the Mishna. In addition, he instituted seven *middot*, or measurements, to study the Talmud. These rules are used to this day.

The Ab Beth Din, or second in command to Hillel, was a sage named Shammai. He too was highly respected, but his views of the laws and his personality were more stringent than those of Hillel. There are many stories concerning differences between Shammai and Hillel. For instance, a heathen came to Shammai and asked, "Can you tell me the whole Torah while I stand on one foot?" Shammai thought the man was making sport of him and drove him away. The man then went to Hillel and asked the same question. Hillel's response: "Do not unto others what you would not have others do unto you. All the rest is commentary." The man was amazed (*Shabbath* 31:1). This became the golden rule for Judaism—a negative formulation of the golden rule given by Jesus in Matthew 7:12.

For the most part, Hillel's rulings were accepted over Shammai's—many believe because of his simplicity, kindness, and humility. According to the Midrash, "The words of both schools are the words of the living God, but the Law follows the ruling of the school of Hillel because the Hillelites were gentle and modest, and studied both their own opinions and opinions of the other school and humbly mentioned the words of the other school before theirs."

One of Hillel's most important rulings concerned forgiveness of debts in the sabbatical (seventh) year. A lender would not lend money if he knew the sabbatical year was near. Hillel did not want to break a command of God, yet circumstances were such that hardships were created. He thus ruled that a loan could be given without being forgiven if a third party, such as a court, collected the money and gave it to the lender. Hillel found a way out.

That "way out" characterizes Hillel's style and Judaism to this very day. It certainly is indicative of another famous statement attributed to Hillel: "If I am not for myself—who is for me? and being for my ownself—what am I? and if not now—when?"

It is important to understand Hillel and his teachings because they give insight into the way Jewish people think religiously. There is no better illustration of this than in the closing paragraph of *The Jewish People*, the elementary history book used in my Hebrew school (italics added):

> Hillel's method of explaining the law *appealed to the people*, and his decisions were accepted everywhere. Not only his own generation, but future generations as well, *lived by the rules Hillel had made*. When times changed, other teachers followed Hillel's method. *They explained the laws so that people could live by the Torah even when conditions changed.*

There is no doubt that Hillel was a knowledgeable, kind, and pious person—a man due great respect. His method of adaptation to the changing times was the prescription for a move toward the only truth. Times certainly change, but God's Word never does.

RAMBAM AND RASHI: BRINGING THE BOTTOM LINE

Often in conversation we are asked, "What's the bottom line?" It is a plea to cut through a plethora of explanations and get to the gist of the matter.

Even before the completion of the Talmud in 50 A.D., there was a need to come to the essence of the massive amount of text so that the scattered Jewish people could better understand their faith.

Separated by time (about one hundred years) and distance (several hundred miles), two men provided the means for the Jewish people to study both the Talmud and the Bible. These *helps* are still used today, not only by many Jewish people, but by Gentiles and Christians as well.

The Rambam

Cordova, Spain, was the birthplace of the first man. Referred to as the "other Moses, Rabbi Moses ben Maimon (*Rambam*) was born in 1135. During his adolescence, he wandered from place to place because of the religious persecutions in Spain and North Africa. During this time, however, the gifted youth satisfied his insatiable appetite for knowledge by reading many books. He became fluent in Hebrew, Arabic, and Spanish, and, in addition to the Talmud and Bible, he mastered such subjects as medicine, philosophy, and science.

His first major contribution to help the Jewish community understand their texts was a work called *Perush Hamishuyot*. Written in Arabic and taking ten years to complete, it simplified huge portions of Mishnaic texts. The 13

principles of faith that are part of this work form a standard
on which Jewish people may base their beliefs. Each begins
with "Ani ma'amin..." ("I believe...") and are as follows:

> I believe that God created all things...that God
> is one...that God does not have a body...that
> God is forever...that Jews must worship God
> alone...that the prophets are inspired by
> God...that Moses was the greatest prophet...that
> God revealed the Torah to Moses...that our
> Torah will never be changed...that God knows
> our secret thoughts...that God rewards those
> who are good and punishes those who are
> evil...that the Messiah will someday come...in
> the resurrection of the dead.

Not only were these principles of great help to the Jews of
Maimonides' day, but millions of Jews recited them as they
marched into the ovens of the Holocaust.

Another tool developed by the Rambam was called the
Mishna Torah. This immense work (14 volumes), written in
Hebrew, took ten years to complete. All the laws of the Torah
are arranged according to subject and are put in a systematic
order. The Mishna came about as a result of a comprehensive
study of Jewish lore, the Talmud, the Midrash, and other rabbinic literature. This work has been very influential in the
Jewish community over the years because of its readability for
both young and old.

While the Rambam's labor of love was religious scholarship,
his life's labor was as a physician. He served as the personal doc-
tor to the royal court of Cairo, which included Saladin and his
son. Maimonides' scholarship was not limited to Judaistic writing. He was also a noteworthy philosopher, and his *Guide to the*

Perplexed is easily the most significant philosophic work of any Jew. Written when he was 55, its goal was to reconcile reason with faith and harmonize Judaism with philosophy. However, with its 176 chapters divided into three parts, it is so vast a work that many people avoid it.

In the year 1204, the Rambam—the one who lived his life to help others, the one of whom it was said, "From Moses to Moses, there is none like Moses"—died. He had become so famous that a public fast was proclaimed in Jerusalem upon news of his death, and it was said of him, "The glory is departed from Israel." Even today, many people visit his grave in the city of Tiberias, Israel.

Rashi

In the unfamiliar village of Troyes, France, another notable Talmudic scholar was born. His name was Solomon ben Isaac. He became known as *Rashi*, taken from his name, Rabbi Shlomo ben Isaac.

Rashi came from very humble means, yet he was able to attend two notable yeshivas. He made his living by running a successful wine business, but his real passion was learning, particularly the Torah and Talmud. While still in his mid-20s, he founded his own yeshiva, where he instructed hundreds of students. For 40 years, he used his tremendous knowledge of the Talmud—both in *Halacha* (*laws*) and *Agodoth* (*narration*)—as well as his extensive knowledge of science and secularism to provide a simplified understanding of the complex text of the Talmud. Rashi was able to take vast numbers of Talmudic texts, which contained neither punctuation nor indication of the speaker, and explain them in short sentences, sometimes even a single word.

Rashi also wrote a commentary on the Bible, covering

every book except Chronicles. It was translated into several languages and has been used not only by Jewish people, but by Gentile and Christian theologians as well. One of the most notable users of his commentary was Protestant reformer Martin Luther. To this very day, young students of religion *cut their teeth* on the work of Rashi.

Although committed Christians and Jews differ on a number of significant areas, there is mutual agreement in one key area. Both have a strong desire to know and understand the Book. The Rambam and Rashi were men of impact, helping their people arrive at the *bottom line* of the volumes of writings that are the basis of their beliefs and traditions. We can thank God that He made His Word readable for even the simplest among us.

HOW TO BE A MENSCH

My mother gasped when she saw me walk through the door after a semester away at college. I had left home clean shaven with short hair, and now—well, let's just say she had trouble finding my face. She took one look at me and cried out, "Oy! Oy! Oy! Why can't you be a *mensch*?"

"What is a mensch?" you ask.

The word *mensch* (rhymes with *bench*) is a Yiddish word. Yiddish is written in Hebrew letters with primarily German vocabulary. Other Yiddish words are taken from languages such as Polish, Romanian, Russian, and Lithuanian. Hundreds of Yiddish words have been adopted into the English language—words such as *chutzpah* (*nerve* or *gall*), *nosh* (*to snack*), *oy vey* (*oh my*), *kvetch* (*to complain*), *shlep* (*to drag*), *kosher* (*fit* or *proper*), *shmooz* (*friendly talk*), and *tsuris* (*trouble*).

My untidy appearance 20 years ago portrayed to my mother the image of a person who lived an improper lifestyle. She wondered why I couldn't look like a human being, the literal translation of *mensch*. The Yiddish language consistently broadens the meaning of its words so that many become difficult to translate. To understand the meaning of *mensch*, let me use a common Jewish tool—storytelling.

Doing What is Right

The first story involves my friend Brian, who owned a successful business. One particular client accounted for the majority of his business. However, unknown to Brian, that client's own business was failing miserably. Keeping up a front, they continued to funnel huge projects to Brian involving large amounts of money. By the time Brian learned that his client was in trouble, it was too late. His client filed for bankruptcy, leaving Brian with incredible debt. He sought advice about how to deal with his financial dilemma and was told to file for bankruptcy himself. This he would not do. Instead, he contacted each of his debtors, explaining what had happened. He told them that he would faithfully repay what he owed them, but he asked for their patience. The response was extremely favorable. It took several years, but he was finally able to pay off his debt to each of them. Brian's behavior was the essence of being a mensch. He did not do what was expedient; he did what was right.

The second story involves a young man named Brad who was born with cerebral palsy. While his body is wracked by the disease, his brainpower is spectacular. He is unable to speak, although he understands three languages. He uses a head pointer to operate his computer, running intricate and sophisticated programs.

Brad makes it a habit to be conscious of circumstances around him. For instance, he became aware of a missionary family in need of an automobile. He puts aside his disability money to assist people he sees in need, so he told his father to be on the lookout for a good used car. It wasn't long before his dad found such a car, and Brad instructed him to purchase it and drive him to the family's home in it. When that family received such a wonderful gift from someone whose circumstances are less than ideal, they were moved to tears. This young man is a real mensch, extending kindness to others while disregarding his own difficulties.

The third story involves a Jewish dentist who lives in the northeast. Irving has practiced dentistry for more than 50 years and has had a long-standing policy that might surprise some people. He provides free dental care to Christian workers. Whenever a Christian worker tries to pay for his services, he always replies, "No charge—because of the work you do." Although Irving does not have the same faith as the Christian workers he helps, he is a mensch because his respect for God moves him to honor those who he believes serve that same God.

In Micah 6:8 the prophet alludes to a mensch: "He hath shown thee, O man, what is good; and what doth the LORD require of thee, but to do justly, and to love mercy, and to walk humbly with thy God?" The prophet clearly states that if people do justly, love mercy, and walk humbly, they are doing the will of God. These stories illustrate individuals who behaved just that way. They were mensches.

For Christians, the ultimate mensch is Jesus the Messiah, who always did the will of His Father. Believers are to model their lives after Christ. Thus, the question my mother asked me should be asked of each Christian: "Are you a mensch?"

ENDNOTES

1 Klapperman, Gilbert and Libby, *The Story of the Jewish People* (New York: Behrman House, Inc., Publishers, 1958), vol. 3, p. 11.

2 Menes, Abraham, *The Jews: Their Religion and Culture*, ed. Louis Finkelstein (New York: Schoken Books, 1971), p. 179.

3 Rosten, Leo, *The Joys of Yiddish* (New York: Pocket Books, 1970), p. 19.

4 *Ibid.*, preface xvi.

5 Patai, Raphael, *The Vanished Worlds of Jewry* (Macmillan Publishing Co., Inc., 1980), p. 10.

6 Rosten, *loc. cit.*

7 Patai, *loc. cit.*

8 Klapperman, *op.cit.*, p. 40.

9 Rudaavsky, David, *Modern Jewish Religious Movements* (New York: Behrman House, Inc., Publishers, 1967), p. 113.

10 Klapperman, *op cit.*, p. 61.

11 *Ibid.*, vol. 4, p. 20.

12 "Israel in the News," source *Newsweek, Israel My Glory*, vol. 49, no. 3, June/July 1991, p. 28.

13 *Chicago Tribune*, October 1990.

14 A conclave of three hundred representatives showed up at the International Federation of Secular Humanistic Jews (*Chicago Tribune*, October 19, 1990).

15 Kertzer, Rabbi Morris N., *What is a Jew?* (New York: Collier Books, Macmillan Publishing Company), 4th ed., pp. 4-5.

16 Varner, Will, "The Messiah of the Common People," *Israel My*

Glory, vol. 46, no. 4, October/November 1988, p. 6; _____, "Another Look at the Pharisees," *Israel My Glory,* vol. 47, no. 3, June/July 1989, p. 10.

[17] Arden, Harvey, "The Pious Ones," *National Geographic,* August 1975.

[18] Bernstein, Rabbi Phillip S., *What the Jews Believe* (New York: Union of Hebrew Congregations, in cooperation with Farrar, Straus, and Young, 1950), p. 13.

[19] *Ibid.*

[20] Limburg, James, *Judaism: An Introduction for Christians* (Minneapolis: Augsburg Publishing House), p. 75.

[21] *Encyclopaedia Judaica,* "Reconstructionism," 16 volumes, p. 1615.

THE JEWISH LIFE CYCLE

BECAUSE IT'S A MITZVAH

When people visit Mea Shearim, one of the most Orthodox communities in all of Israel, or observe the crowds gathered at the Western Wall of Herod's Temple in Jerusalem, questions often arise: What motivates people to be so committed? Why do some people shun leaven for eight days each spring? Why do some eat their meals in a portable structure made of branches during the feast of Succoth? What motivates them to fast each year on Yom Kippur? Moving into the secular world, Jewish parents who want to see their children exhibit a particular behavior could also be asked, Why?

The answer in each of these situations can best be stated in three words—words my mother often used to get me to do something or not to do something. In fact, she still uses them today, given the opportunity. She would tell me, "Do this...go there...don't do that...because IT'S A *MITZVAH!*" Inevitably, those three words would freeze me, even if only for an instant, because *mitzvot* (plural) are at the heart of Judaism.

Mitzvah is defined in a number of ways. In its simplest form, a mitzvah is a command given by God; it is a divine precept. The definition has been expanded to include anything that promotes proper behavior. That change came about because the word *mitzvah* has also been translated to mean *charity.* Thus, another definition for mitzvah is *good deed.* Whether Orthodox, Conservative, or Reform, many Jewish people believe that performing a mitzvah is a means of purifying themselves, thus providing great satisfaction in doing *the right thing.*

There are 613 mitzvot in the Jewish Scriptures (Old Testament). They are divided into the "Thou shalts"—248 positive commandments that correspond in number to the parts of the human body—and the "Thou shalt nots"—365 negative commandments that correspond in number to the days of the solar year. They are also divided into three types of commandments. The first type is called *hukim* or *statutes.* Hukim are given by God, and their purposes are often difficult to understand. For example, it is prohibited to combine wool with linen in a garment (Deuteronomy 22:11). The second type is called *mishpatim,* which are *judgments.* These commands should be followed, even if the command from God did not exist. They consist of such things as honoring one's parents, not stealing, or not murdering. The third division of laws, called *edot,* relates to being a visible witness to others, such as keeping Passover or wearing the *tallit (prayer shawl).*

While the triple division of mitzvot is God-given, there is an additional threefold division of mitzvot that is man-made. The first division is called *minhag.* These laws started as customs. The customs eventually became ingrained in the Jewish life experience and were just as binding as any Jewish law. An example of a minhag is religious men wearing the *yarmulke* (*skull cap*). The second division is called *gezeirah*. These laws were established by great sages to protect people from breaking the laws of the Scriptures. An example of a gezeirah is not touching a pen on the Sabbath because the law says not to write on that day. The last division of man-made mitzvot is called *takkanah*. These were created to help the general welfare of people within their communities and include such requirements as establishing elementary schools or drawing up a *ketuba* (*marriage contract*) to guarantee that a husband meets his obligations to his wife.

It is impossible for any person to obey all 613 biblical mitzvot because not all laws apply to all people. For instance, some laws relate only to the priests, who are of the tribe of Levi. Other laws involve the Temple, which at present does not exist. Still others exempt women because of their obligation to raise the family, a task involving a significant amount of time. In addition, it is believed that, by their very nature, men need more restrictions or restraints than women, who are regarded as more spiritually minded. One rabbi of recent times has taken all of these variables into account and estimates that the average person could follow 271 biblical mitzvot. He broke these down into 77 positive laws and 194 negative commands.

Surprisingly, Judaism teaches seven mitzvot that should be observed by Gentiles. These were given to Noah after the flood to be passed down through his sons. They are as follows: Believe in the one true God; do not blaspheme; do not kill; do not steal; do not be sexually immoral; set up courts of law; do not eat the flesh of an animal that was cut from it while it was still alive.

All these facts about mitzvot still do not explain the motivation behind performing them. Jewish people perform mitzvot to assure a right standing with the God of the universe. According to Judaism, each fall on Yom Kippur, the Day of Atonement, the good and bad deeds done by people throughout the year are weighed by God. The ten days between Rosh Hashanah (the Jewish New Year) and Yom Kippur are known as the Days of Awe. During these ten days, Jewish people try to perform as many mitzvot as possible to insure that their names will be sealed in the Book of Life for the coming year. But people never know if they have done enough.

The words of my mother—"Because it's a mitzvah!"—motivated me to a given action. Now, as a follower of the Messiah, I know God's Word is clear. "All our righteousnesses are as filthy rags" (Isaiah 64:6). "For there is not a just man upon   earth, that doeth good and sinneth not" (Ecclesiastes 7:20). "For by grace are ye saved through faith; and that not of yourselves, it is the gift of God—Not of works, lest any man should boast" (Ephesians 2:8-9).

Thoughtful observers must ponder their own motivations for action. Do we perform good deeds to achieve a good standing with God? Or do we rest in the finished work of Christ on our behalf and desire to win others by our love and good deeds?

BRIT MILAH

The birth of a boy into a Jewish family is cause for great joy and celebration (*simcha*). On the eighth day after his birth, a ceremony takes place that unites him with all other Jewish males in a bond of commitment to the God of Israel. It is a rite of passage so important that, if not obeyed, is seen as a rejection of Judaism itself. Called the covenant of circumcision (*Brit Milah*), it is the physical removal of the foreskin. This covenant is the oldest of Jewish rites, and its inception dates back to the time when God gave it to Abraham (Genesis 17:9-14).

Specified in the covenant are several requirements made to Abraham and his future seed. First, a sign was needed as proof that a promise was made: "and it shall be a sign of the covenant between me and you" (v. 11). Second, the sign was given to every male child who reached a specific age: "And he that is eight days old shall be circumcised among you" (v. 12). Third, it involved all future offspring of Abraham: "Thou shalt keep my covenant...and thy seed after thee in their generations" (v. 9). Fourth, an "uncircumcised male child whose flesh of his foreskin is not circumcised, that soul shall be cut off from his people; he hath broken my covenant" (v. 14). Finally, the covenant was to be eternal: "my covenant shall be in your flesh for an everlasting covenant" (v. 13).

Over the centuries, a body of Jewish tradition has developed around the rite of Brit. It is assumed that Adam, created in perfect fellowship with God, was made without a foreskin. Others say Abraham was circumcised on the 10th day of the month of Tishri and, later in history, that date was ordained by God to be the Day of Atonement. On that day, sin, the cause of division between God and man, was to be dealt with. Still another tradition practiced by many today involves placing an empty chair at the ceremony to await the spirit of Elijah who, according to the Talmudic interpretation of 1 Kings 19:10, attends and witnesses every circumcision.

Although Jewish liturgy is amazingly diverse in its celebration of the Brit, there are many unifying factors. First, as in the days of Abraham, a Brit is performed on the eighth day after birth. A baby born on the Sabbath (Saturday) is circumcised the following Sabbath. The only thing that can prevent a Brit being performed on the eighth day is the ill health of the baby. Second, fathers today have the same responsibility to circumcise their sons as did Abraham of old. But, rather than perform the surgery themselves, fathers today often use the services of a *Mohel*, who is specially trained in the surgical procedure and has a thorough knowledge of the Jewish law regarding circumcision.

During the ceremony, the baby is held by a person of honor, called the *Sandek*, who is chosen by the father. If called for, the *Sandek* may serve as the child's godfather. The ceremony is brief and often includes many family members, although the primary participants are the baby, his father, the Mohel, and the Sandek. A blessing is given as the baby is brought in, and prayers are recited by the Mohel, the Sandek, and the father. The Sandek continues to hold the baby as he is given his formal Hebrew name. After the surgery is completed, the blessing over the wine (*kiddush*) is recited. Also, the Mohel usually places gauze soaked in wine in the baby's mouth as an anesthetic. All prayers recited during the ceremony are directed to the "King of the universe," with the desire that the child be obedient, love the Torah, be fruitful, and do good deeds.

Many medical facts attest to the advantages of circumcision for cleanliness and lowered cancer rates. Medical science has also demonstrated that the eighth day after birth is a prime time for the clotting of blood. But despite these practical reasons, the basis for the Brit is to carry out the command of God in the covenant He made with Abraham to set aside a people for Himself.

Moses used the covenant of circumcision to illustrate what God must do for every person who desires to have a relationship with Him: "And the LORD thy God will circumcise thine heart, and the heart of thy seed, to love the LORD thy God with all thine heart, and with all thy soul, that thou mayest live" (Deuteronomy 30:6). Physical circumcision does not guarantee a good relationship with God. Moses said that to love God, God must perform spiritual surgery on the heart. Our heavenly Father does the work of a Mohel and performs spiritual surgery on the heart of every believer. When people place their trust in Jesus Christ, they are circumcised "with the circumcision made without hands, in putting off the body of the sins of the flesh by the circumcision of Christ" (Colossians 2:11).

BAR MITZVAH

On Saturday morning, June 11, 1966, I walked from the stage of the synagogue to the platform *(bema)* where the Torah lay open. Following in the tradition of my father and grandfather, I had prepared for this event since early childhood. As it had for multitudes before me, the event signaled a change in my standing in the Jewish community. I would no longer be considered innocent, for I would take on full religious responsibility. I would no longer be considered a child, for, at the moment when I read from the Holy Scripture, I became a man in the traditions of Judaism. That day marked my *bar mitzvah,* the day I became a *son of commandment.*

A religious rite practiced by the Jewish people as far back as the 13th century, the concept of the bar mitzvah can be traced to the pages of the Talmud. It was there that religious accountability was bestowed when a boy was physically becoming a man. The Jewish Scriptures know no such rite. The only age of accountability found in the Torah is in the first chapter of Numbers, where all men 20 years and older were counted for service in the army. Today, the bar mitzvah is one of the most important events in the life of a Jewish man.

Most bar mitzvahs today involve a synagogue service and a reception. Actually, the ceremony involves three parts: the *Release* (called *Shepetarni*), the *Sermon* (called *Derashah)*, and the *Meal* (called the *Seudah*). The emphasis on any or all of these parts is determined by the family and therefore varies from one family to the next.

The release involves the bar mitzvah boy and his father. To begin, the father prays, "Blessed be He who has relieved me of this obligation" (Midrash Genesis 63:10). Henceforth, all the improprieties and sins the young man commits will fall on him and not on his father. Next, the young man receives the call *(aliya)* to the bema to read from the Torah (the five books of Moses) and the Haftorah (the prophets). He also recites various blessings as he leads the congregation in worship. As the boy reads in flawless Hebrew, his father, mother, and the remainder of his family *kvell* (look on with pride), doubtless reflecting on the months and years of preparation that have culminated in this day.

Over the years, the Derashah has changed from a sermon, or expounding over the Scriptures and Talmud, to a speech in which the bar mitzvah boy thanks his parents and the others who have helped him arrive at this event in his life. The change reflects a sad trend away from the demonstration of a capable young man handling the Scriptures and the Writings to a recognition of family to the invited guests.

The third part of the ceremony, the festive meal, was originally a simple time of refreshment and celebration. Today parties—complete with dance halls, bands, and elaborate catered meals—are more the rule than the exception. Some rabbis have commented that they see more *bar* (drinking) than *mitzvah* (commands or good deeds). During this time gifts are given to the young man in recognition of his achievement. At the time my father and his peers celebrated their bar mitzvahs (in the 1920s and 1930s), a fountain pen was a common yet outstanding gift, symbolizing adulthood. Today it is not uncommon for the bar mitzvah boy to receive thousands of dollars, a healthy boost for his college fund.

Once he has become a son of commandment, the young man has four privileges bestowed upon him. First, he is counted with the men to make up a *minyan* (the group of ten men needed to conduct a service of public worship). Second, he puts on *phylacteries* (two small square leather boxes containing slips inscribed with scriptural passages and worn on the left arm and the head) each morning for the rest of his life as he recites the morning prayers. Third, he can be called upon at any time to go up *(aliya)* to read from the Torah. Fourth, he can now be a part of the Jewish court (*bet din*). Although these privileges are now part of his life, the young man probably will not exercise them, with the exception of the minyan. The majority of Jewish men cease from synagogue activity upon completion of their bar mitzvahs.

For many Jewish families, the bar mitzvah is very important. It is not uncommon for families to fly to Israel to celebrate the occasion there. Bar mitzvah services take place at the Wailing Wall (or Western Wall) every Monday and Thursday, and Jews from around the world can be seen in the joyous celebrations. Many Israeli Jews celebrate their bar mitzvahs at Masada, a fortress in the Judean desert that symbolizes Jewish freedom and determination.

Conservative and Reform Jews have broadened the bar mitzvah to include girls. Because girls mature faster than boys, the *bat mitzvah* (*daughter of commandment*) is celebrated when a girl turns 12. There are no bat mitzvahs in Israel, where the state religion is Orthodox.

The original purpose of a bar mitzvah was to recognize the years of training in the Word and to celebrate another man now able to understand and devote himself to the Scriptures. With this background, we can gain insight into the importance of training a child in the way he should go (Proverbs 22:6) and, perhaps, be encouraged in the raising of our own families.

THE JEWISH WEDDING

Marriage is regarded as one of the most important and significant decisions in the lives of Jewish people. The Torah clearly states that God made "an help fit" for Adam because "It is not good that the man should be alone" (Gen. 2:18). Acknowledging God's truth, the great Jewish sages taught that marriage was part of the divine plan of God. They permitted the suspension of Torah study to attend a wedding and allowed the selling of a Torah scroll to gain the means to marry. The Talmud states that without a wife, a man has no joy, happiness, or bliss. Some statements from the sages of old question the humanity of a man who does not marry.

No details are given in the Scripture regarding the actual marriage ceremony, but we do know of four of its elements: the betrothal period (Deuteronomy 20:7), which lasts for a full year; singing—beautiful, romantic singing (Song of Solomon 4:1-7); one week or feasting (Genesis 29:22); and the consummation of the marriage (Genesis 29:23, 30).

The Talmud details the ceremony, providing guidelines regarding age, days, eligibility, and procedure. With so many important things to consider, it is no wonder that the profession of matchmaker was most prominent. It is said that it is as difficult for God to arrange a good marriage as it was to split the Red Sea.

Long ago, a year separated the betrothal from the consummation, allowing the groom to prepare the home and the bride to validate her virginity. Today, these stages are combined into one ceremony called *kiddushin.*

On the Sabbath before the wedding, the groom is "called up" (*aliya*) to the *bema* (*platform*) to read the Torah. The congregation showers him with candies, representing wishes for a sweet married life. Other preparations include the bride purchasing a *tallit* for her husband-to-be and a period of fasting by the couple, signifying their sorrow for sin and their desire for a new beginning. The man and woman separately immerse themselves into the ritual bath called the *mikveh*, which is a bath of natural water instituted for the purpose of sanctification. As they immerse themselves, they proclaim their devotion to one another and separation from others.

When they arrive at the synagogue, the bride and groom sign a *ketuba*, or *marriage contract*. This document, written in Aramaic, is a religious contract binding the groom to fulfill all financial duties to his wife. The private signing of the ketuba is witnessed by two people who must be present at the public reading during the ceremony.

The wedding ceremony begins as the veiled bride walks toward her groom, usually escorted by both of her parents. At the front of the aisle, the couple stands together under the *chupah (bridal canopy.)* The bride's procession to this point represents her walk to the new home the groom has prepared for her. The canopy represents the couple's new home, as well as the establishment of their home together. As they stand under the canopy, the rabbi recites a blessing over the wine, hallowing the name of God and blessing the marriage.

The rabbi then reads the ketuba and the marriage vows, which are repeated by the couple. The groom places an unadorned ring on the bride's right index finger (the most visible) and declares, "You are consecrated unto me with this ring in accordance with the laws of Moses and Israel." At a later time, the groom places the ring on the traditional ring finger, from which, it is believed, a vein runs straight to the heart. Seven blessings *(sheva berachot)* are recited to bless and thank God for the wine, creation, the creation of man, man's creation in the image of God, the future return of God's chosen to Zion, the bride and groom, and the joy of all weddings.

It is traditional for the groom to stand on the left and the bride to his right, as the Scriptures state, "upon thy right hand did stand the queen" (Psalm 45:9). The bride then circles her groom, sometimes alone, sometimes accompanied by her mother, his mother, and her bridesmaids.

As the ceremony concludes, the groom breaks a wine glass by smashing it with his foot, as the guests shout, "*Mazel tov!*" *(good luck)*. The breaking of the glass is said to signify sorrow over the destruction of the Temple. Another interpretation is that the smashing of the glass is irrevocable and permanent; so too may the marriage last for all time.

In many services, a time is then set aside for the couple to be alone together to reflect on what has just taken place. This is taken from the biblical pattern (Genesis 29:22-23), when the couple actually consummated their marriage. Finally, a reception is held to congratulate the newlyweds and celebrate their union.

Just as marriage is important in the eyes of Judaism, so it should be very significant to true believers. We, the church, are the bride of the Savior and soon-coming Messiah, the Lord Jesus Christ, who is our groom.

DEATH AND MOURNING

Chai is the Hebrew word for *life*. Jewish people frequently wear gold charms depicting this Hebrew character on chains around their necks, emphasizing the fact that life is Judaism's most precious and cherished commodity. Although Judaic doctrine holds that death is the "doorway to the world to come," few Jewish people think or hear much about this perspective. On the contrary, death's sting is very sharp, and death is a difficult thing to handle in the Jewish experience. At the time of death, two considerations must be given priority. First, the utmost respect must be shown for the lifeless body, and second, care and concern must be shown for the mourners.

Interment must be accomplished as soon as possible after death, preferably within 24 hours. Delay is permissible on the Sabbath or to await the arrival of relatives. Embalming is not generally performed. Removing the blood is considered mutilation, a sign of disrespect. Autopsies are also forbidden unless another life can be saved thereby or if civil law deems it necessary. If an autopsy is performed, the body must be restored as much as possible. Cremation is also considered improper, for it violates Genesis 3:19, "dust thou art, and unto dust shalt thou return."

As soon as possible after death occurs, the body is washed and covered with a plain, pocketless white shroud, symbolizing equality. Death visits all—rich or poor, old or young, male or female. If the deceased is a male, a *tallit* (*prayer shawl*) is draped over him. Although the immediate family may request a viewing, public display of the body is discouraged. Some feel that it shows disrespect, whereas others believe it is better to have the last sight of a person while he or she is alive.

Before the start of a funeral service, a cut (*keria*) is made in the clothing of immediate family members. This ritual rending of the garment recalls the practice of the patriarchs as a display of great grief. Many funeral homes provide black scarves that have been cut and can be worn or pinned to clothing so that an actual garment does not have to be damaged. If parents are mourning a child, the left side of the cloth is cut because the left side is closest to the heart. The cut is made on the right side of the cloth when mourning all other immediate family members. *Keria* is observed for seven days.

Flowers are not displayed nor is any music played at a Jewish funeral. The sweet smell of the flowers and the pleasing sound of instruments are forbidden pleasures during this time. If the deceased had any special requests for the funeral, they are honored, provided that they do not violate Jewish law.

At the grave, *a minyan (ten men)* is required to recite the *kaddish,* which is an Aramaic word meaning *holy.* It is not a prayer for the dead, as some suppose, but rather a poem that exalts the name of God. It reads, in part, "Magnified and sanctified be His great name in the world which He created according to His will....Blessed, praised and glorified, exalted, extolled and honored, adored and lauded be the name of the Holy One." The family recites kaddish from the day of the funeral until the 11th month. The mourners proclaim through the kaddish the marvel, wonder, and exaltation of the living God in the midst of terrible grief. A simple pine box (more easily decomposed) containing the body is lowered into the ground. The family takes turns shoveling dirt into the grave until the grave is filled. A grave marker is not displayed until the first anniversary of the death. This special service is called the "stone setting" or "unveiling."

Three periods of mourning are observed. The first is called *shiva (seven).* It starts upon arrival home from the funeral and lasts for seven days. All immediate family members—parents, spouses, children, and siblings—observe shiva. They sit on low stools, wear house slippers, and refrain from enjoyable activities. At the home, the first meal the family partakes of after the funeral is prepared and served by friends. This is considered a *mitzvah* (*good deed*) because the family is too grief stricken to prepare the meal. Egg dishes are common at this meal because eggs symbolize the life cycle. Condolences are encouraged during this week-long period. Donations toward disease research or the synagogue or the planting of a tree in Israel are common memorials given. *Shloshim* (*thirty*) is the second period of mourning. Music, parties, and weddings should not be part of the mourner's experience during this time. The third period, observed for a father or mother, is called *avelut* and lasts for one year after the death.

Every year on the anniversary of the death a candle is lit to remember the deceased. This practice is called *yahrzeit* and is explained by Proverbs 20:27, "The spirit of man is the lamp of the LORD, searching all the inward parts." For those Jewish people who do not believe in life after death, this practice is particularly significant. Through it they are remembered by their loved ones, thus assuring them a form of immortality.

Death is a robber, insidious and frightening unless there is real hope beyond the grave. The Apostle Paul looked death in the eye and recorded these words: "O death, where is thy sting? O grave, where is thy victory?" (1 Corinthians 15:55). The Messiah of Israel won the victory when He went through "the valley of the shadow of death" (Psalm 23:4) in our place.

JEWISH WORSHIP

THE SHEMA:
HOW MUCH OF ME DOES GOD OWN?

Hear, O Israel: The LORD our God is one LORD:
And thou shalt love the LORD thy God with all thine
heart, and with all thy soul, and with all thy might.
And these words, which I command thee this day,
shall be in thine heart; And thou shalt teach them diligently unto thy children, and shalt talk of them when
thou sittest in thine house, and when thou walkest by
the way, and when thou liest down, and when thou
risest up. And thou shalt bind them for a sign upon
thine hand, and they shall be as frontlets between
thine eyes. And thou shalt write them upon the posts
of thy house, and on thy gates (Deuteronomy. 6:4-9).

The young man, still a teenager, performed a number of rituals each day. The first was to deliver the daily newspaper. He got up very early, delivered the papers, and returned home before the rest of the family was even awake. Then, just as the sun was rising, he would wrap the long black leather strap of his *tefillin* around his left arm. At the end of the strap was a tiny wooden box, which he positioned so that it pointed to his heart. A second tiny wood box was placed between his eyes and secured with two leather straps tied behind his head. With these in place, and a *yarmulke* covering his head, he put his *tallis* over his shoulders. Now he was ready to pray:

Shema Yisroel! Adonoi Elohenu, Adonoi Echod....

The Shema (pronounced Sh'MAH): What is this prayer that is recited daily by observant Jews? What is the meaning of these Hebrew words that even the most secular Jew likely remembers from his childhood?

The Shema is probably the one aspect of Judaism with which all Jews identify. The Shema is from the Torah, found in Deuteronomy 6:4-9. It is not so much a prayer as a statement:

Hear, O Israel: The LORD our God, the LORD is one.

Rabbi Hayim Halevy Donin calls it a "declaration of faith."[1] The Shema links Jews together. The Shema is the most important prayer Jewish people can pray. It can, however, be the statement that keeps them from a relationship with the Messiah when it should be the one that causes them to look for Him.

Reciting the Shema

I was that young man who prayed faithfully each morning. I was less faithful with the evening ritual, even though it was equally important. The Bible says it should be said "when thou liest down, and when thou risest up" (Deuteronomy 6:7). It is to be recited with great respect. We are talking to the Almighty God, who is not to be taken lightly. Many Jewish people say the prayer with their eyes closed, to concentrate and focus on the King of the universe. The *Encyclopaedia Judaica* tells us that the followers of Rabbi Shammai taught that the Shema should be said standing in the morning and lying down in the evening. According to the school of Rabbi Hillel, the man's position was not important so long as he recited the Shema twice a day.[2] Today most people would agree that what is important is that it is said, without regard to a person's physical stance while saying it.

The important principle of the Shema is that it incorporates the concept of the whole man. Numbers have always held great significance for the Jewish people. Rabbis have added the three words *el melekh*, and *ne'eman* (*God, king,* and *faithful*) to the existing 245 words of the prayer, bringing the total to 248. According to Jewish tradition, a human being is made up of 248 parts. Thus, the Shema is for the whole person.

Reciting the Shema is not a problem for most Jewish people because most have it memorized. I knew it in kindergarten. No, reciting it is not the problem. Fulfilling the requirements of the Shema is usually more difficult.

Requirements of the Shema ─────────────

Truly fulfilling the precepts of the Shema requires an unparalleled commitment.

   ...thou shalt love the LORD *thy God....*

Exodus 21:2-6 tells us that a slave could be set free after six years of service. However, if, for the security of his family or his love for his master, he wanted to stay in service, provision was made to do that. The passage goes on to say that the master would pierce the slave's ear with an awl, making him his servant for life. The love of this slave for his master was thus shown to be very powerful. When a Jewish person recites the Shema, whether he knows it or not, he is talking about a powerful love. In a sense, it is this picture of slave love, a desire to commit oneself to another for life. The commitment is based on love.

...thou shalt love the LORD thy God with all thine heart....

In Hebrew, the word *labab* has the idea of will or intention. In other words, I must love God with all my *will*.

...soul.... The Hebrew word *nephesh* has the idea of life. I must love Him with my *life*.

...might.... This Hebrew word is *mo'ed*. I must love God with all my *strength*.

J. McBride, as quoted in the *Theological Word Book of the Old Testament*, said, "The three parts of Deuteronomy 6:5 rather than signifying different spheres of biblical psychology, seem to be semantically concentric. They were chosen to reinforce the absolute devotion to God."

And these words...shall be in thine heart.

It is clear, then, that the person who prays this prayer and means what he says would want to give his whole self to God, to hold nothing back. God would own him—body, soul, and spirit. Contrary to an over-used line popular when I was in high school, love does not mean "never having to say you're sorry." Rather, if I have given myself over completely to someone, I would want to ask forgiveness immediately if I hurt that person. Not to do so would mean I have only a passing interest, or none at all.

And thou shalt teach them diligently unto thy children....

A second requirement of the Shema is an undaunted compulsion. Moses said that these words should be taught diligently. The Hebrew word for *diligence* means *to sharpen.* The procedure for sharpening a blade of any kind requires going over it again, and again, and again, and again. When teaching our children about our commitment to God, we are compelled to repeat it time and again, patiently and lovingly.

We should also be talking about our commitment. In Hebrew school we learned that the Talmud teaches that every person has only so many words to speak. The teacher said that when your words are used up, you are dead. This bothered me, and I said, not to be funny, "If this is so, I would have been dead already!" Our commitment is to be so strong that God is always on our lips.

... and shalt talk of them when thou sittest in thine house....

This instruction refers to our time. We have more leisure time than any other civilization in history. We should be using that time to speak of God and His commands.

...and when thou walkest by the way....

We do so many things "by the way." We have our jobs, our families, our sports, our hobbies, and yet we are told that God is the person we should be talking about.

...and when thou liest down, and when thou risest up.

God should be on our lips throughout the day. He is to be taught about and talked about.

And thou shalt bind them [the words] *for a sign upon thine hand, and they shall be as frontlets between thine eyes.*

The Jewish person literally binds the Scripture to his arm and head with the leather straps of his *tefillin.* They are a sign of his commitment.

And thou shalt write them upon the posts of thy house, and on thy gates.

In Jewish households even today, a *mezuza* (a small metal box containing the Shema) is nailed to the doorpost, a sign of the family's commitment to their Jewish traditions.

Reflecting on the Shema

Reciting the requirements of the Shema is never enough. We must reflect on them. Deuteronomy 30:14 tells us that the Word of God is near to them (the Jewish people). This is very true. It is read in the synagogue, it may be bound as a sign, it may be posted on the door, it may even be on a bookshelf in a Jewish household. Most Jewish people know the Shema, if nothing else, by heart. But unless they have a personal relationship with the Messiah of Israel, the Word is not in their hearts. The prophets say that the Jewish people have eyes to see, but they don't see; ears to hear, but they don't hear; hearts to understand, but they don't understand (cp. Isaiah 6:9; Jeremiah 5:21; Ezekiel 12:2).

Many Jewish people wear a necklace with the Hebrew letter *chai* (*life*) on it. For the religious person, *life* means loving God. Loving God means listening to His Word. The Apostle Paul wrote in his second letter to the Corinthians that the Word of God is read to this day, yet a veil covers their eyes (2 Corinthians 3:14).

What about us, Christian friend? We are taught about God. We have Sunday school, Sunday morning services, Sunday evening services, and mid-week prayer meetings. We talk about what God has done in our lives. Our bookstores bulge with available material. All of this is good.

But there is more! We can learn from our observant Jewish friends and their commitment. They are not ashamed of what they are. They let the world know in a tangible way. Yet they don't have the reality of God. They have the outside, but not the inside. Many of us, however, know the reality of God; our hearts understand, but we don't let the world see. Is your love for God so strong that you will bind His Word and teach, talk, and write about Him for everyone to see? Do your neighbors know from outward signs that you are a Christian, just as we would know an observant Jew if we saw one?

We tell our Jewish friends that if they love God with all their heart, soul, and mind, they should be ready to do what He asks in His Word. We tell our Christian friends that if they love God with all their heart, soul, and mind, they should be ready to put their commitment into action.

Let Him examine our commitment. May we prove worthy for His sake.

A LITTLE SANCTUARY

As a youngster growing up, I can remember two synagogues in our neighborhood. Sitting high on a hill was an imposing, three-story brick building with beautiful white stone pillars in the front. It was not called a synagogue but, rather, a temple, after the Temple in Jerusalem that was destroyed. It was progressive and liberal and considered to be on the cutting edge of Conservative/Reform Judaism. It was the synagogue of choice for the majority of young Jewish families. The other synagogue was physically plain, numerically small, and had an elderly congregation. Its doctrine was Orthodox or traditional. This was the synagogue to which my family belonged, and I still hold many fond memories of that place.

Synagogues can vary in doctrine, size, and membership. The thing they have in common is their purpose—to provide a place for Jewish people to worship and assemble.

Synagogues originated around 586 B.C. in Babylon during the years of captivity. After the Temple in Jerusalem was destroyed in 70 A.D. and the people scattered, a tremendous need arose for Jews to gather with one another, read the Torah, and pray. The word *synagogue* comes from the Greek and means to *assemble*. Such assemblies began to spring up wherever large populations of Jewish people were found around the world.

Synagogues were not designed to take the place of the Temple that stood on Mount Moriah in Jerusalem. There was no priesthood established, and no sacrifices were performed. Synagogues were meeting places for the people. When Herod's Temple was destroyed, the synagogue became known to many as the "little sanctuary" (Ezekiel 11:16).

Three Hebrew names or titles are attributed to the synagogue. First is *Bet ha-Midrash* or *house of learning,* because it is the focal point for Jewish education. Hebrew school, Sunday or Sabbath school, and individual training for Bar/Bat Mitzvah are offered on a regular basis. Hebrew, Jewish history, and Bible are taught for adults, and seminars are conducted on such topics as marriage, parenting, and current events.

The second title is *Bet ha-K'nesset*, or *house of assembly*. The synagogue is used by its member families to celebrate *simchas* or *joys*, including wedding receptions, Bar/Bat Mitzvahs, and other special events. Women's groups (sisterhood) and men's groups host their meetings there.

The third title is *Bet ha-Tefillah*, or *house of prayer*. The desire to worship the God of Abraham, Isaac, and Jacob as a group is met in the synagogue. A minimum of ten men (*a minyan*)—or, in some places, women—is all that is required to conduct a service.

Synagogues are autonomous and independent. They are formed, maintained, and controlled locally by the members. Officers are elected to fill various needs—spiritual, educational, or social. Membership is voluntary but does require a fee, which is established by a board. To accommodate all who wish to join, many synagogues offer a sliding financial scale. Donations come in as memorials for special events or for deceased loved ones. In addition, seats are sold for high holy days, and in some synagogues a once-a-year fund raiser is held. Together, these efforts bring in the funds to meet the budgetary needs of the synagogue. As a rule, offerings are not taken in synagogues.

The *rabbi* (*teacher*) is the leader of the synagogue. Originally the rabbi was a member of the community who was extremely knowledgeable and pious, but today he is most likely seminary trained and thus able to administrate, educate, and officiate at special events. The presence of a rabbi is not required for the congregation to gather in worship.

Most synagogues have a *chazan*, or *cantor*, a person who is qualified to lead the congregation in prayer and various Hebrew chants. The *shammas* (*sexton* or *servant*) cares for the property and religious objects used in the synagogue. The president oversees the board, and the treasurer writes the checks and directs the distribution of the finances.

Certain standard objects are found inside a synagogue. The holy ark (*aron kodesh*) is a cabinet in which the Torah scrolls are kept. Above the ark hangs an eternal light (*ner tamid*), as commanded by God in Exodus 27:20-21. The *bema* or *raised platform* is the place from which worship is directed and the Torah is read. Most synagogues are built so that the congregation faces east (toward Jerusalem) when they pray.

I encourage Christians to visit a synagogue service. Whether you go on your own or ask a Jewish friend to take you, you will be warmly received. Perhaps as Christians visit synagogues, they will be made aware of the fact that the missing element in Jewish worship is the person of the Messiah Jesus. "But even unto this day, when Moses is read, the veil is upon their heart" (2 Corinthians 3:15).

DRESSED FOR WORSHIP
PART I: THE TALLIT

Who hasn't had it happen—a missed appointment, that lack of association between a name and a face, the forgotten anniversary or birthday? Forgetfulness is a plague that knows no prejudice. That's why everything from a string tied around a finger to *Post-It Notes* have been used to combat this insidious tormentor.

God, knowing that forgetfulness is just one of many human deficiencies, has given various memory aids—memorials— throughout His Word. These include special feasts, special foods, and even special clothing. When understood and properly used, these memorials serve as reminders of God's provision, power, and person.

In the Torah we read,

> Speak unto the children of Israel, and bid them
> that they make them fringes in the borders of their
> garments throughout their generations, and that
> they put upon the fringe of the borders a cord of
> blue: And it shall be unto you for a fringe, that ye
> may look upon it, and remember all the com-
> mandments of the LORD, and do them; and that
> ye seek not after your own heart and your own
> eyes, after which ye used to play the harlot; That
> ye may remember, and do all my commandments,
> and be holy unto your God (Numbers 15:38-40).

And again, "Thou shalt make thee fringes upon the four quarters of thy vesture, wherewith thou coverest thyself"
(Deuteronomy 22:12).

A brief look at this garment reminds observant Jews of all
the commandments. With 613 commandments to remember,
this particular memory aid has become a graphic visual, absolutely essential to Jewish worship.

This unusual yet attractive garb came to be known as a *tallit* (pronounced tah-LEET). Made of wool or linen with blue
or black stripes, the tallit has tasseled fringes (*tzitziot)* hanging
from each of its four corners. It is these fringes that are biblical. The tallit is merely the medium to hold them. Originally
worn as an outer garment, today it is primarily worn by men
(and women in reform congregations) as a prayer shawl during
public and private worship.

Blue stripes are a reminder of the single blue thread used in
each of the four tassels. No longer used today, this blue thread
was part of the Torah command to include "a cord of blue."
Some choose a tallit with black stripes for one of several possible

reasons. First, the original recipe for making the blue dye was lost with the inhabitants of Akko (Acre) in Israel. Second, when the Romans occupied Palestine, only royalty was permitted to wear the color blue. Third, it is appropriate for mourning since the destruction of the Temple in 70 A.D.

The ancient sages considered several ways in which the fringes aid in remembering all the commandments. One possiblilty is that the word *tzitziot* has the numerical value of 600, which, when added to the eight threads and five knots in each of the tassels, makes a total of 613. Another possibility is that the 608 strands of thread added to the five knots in each of the tassels adds up to 613. Regardless of the actual reason, this commandment is so important to many observant Jews that they wear a *tallit katan (small tallit)* under the shirt, so that the fringes may be displayed at all times. This, they believe, carries out the command, "that ye may look upon it."

How and when a tallit is worn varies among the different cultures of Jewish people. Most men first don a tallit at the time of bar mitzvah, while a few wait until their wedding day. Some drape it over their heads, believing that it improves concentration during prayer. Others wear it merely as a shawl. Many twirl one of the fringes around a finger, kiss it, and then touch the Torah as it is carried around the synagogue during a worship service. All then recite the prayer, "Blessed art thou, O Lord our God, King of the universe, who hast sanctified us by thy commandments, and hast commanded us to wrap ourselves in the fringed garment." Many men are wrapped in tallits for burial. A tear is then made in one of the fringes, symbolizing the end of their obligation to observe the law.

Jesus no doubt wore a tallit, as it was the everyday outer garment common in His day. According to the gospel writers, many people were healed by touching the "border of his garment [*tzitziot*]" (eg., Mark 6:56; Luke 8:44). They were not healed by any supernatural power of the fringes but by the authority of the one wearing them. Some Jewish men have misused this God-given command by enlarging their fringes as a sign of their great spirituality (Matthew 23:5).

Believers are under no obligation to don the tallit because Jesus Christ fulfilled the law. Instead, believers are asked to put on several other things, including the new man created in right-eousness, the whole armor of God, kindness, humility of mind, meekness, long-suffering, and charity. Paul said it best in Galatians 3:27: "For as many of you as have been baptized into Christ have put on Christ." May we never forget everything He has done for us.

PART 2: THE TEFILLIN

As Tevya, the milkman in Sholem Aleichem's story *Fiddler on the Roof,* considered various practices unique to his Judaism, he turned to the audience and asked, "Why do we do the things we do?" And, stroking his beard contemplatively, he answered his own question with a simplistic yet profound explanation: "In one word—tradition!" For years, tradition has been the corner-stone of many Jewish practices. It has been woven into Judaism like a thread into fine fabric.

Daily, at first light (except on the Sabbath and high holy days), Orthodox males (and in some cases, females) don the traditional religious garb, always making sure to put the items in just the right places, in just the right order. Each worship experience serves as an opportunity to identify afresh with their people and their God.

Judaism teaches that the thing used most often is put on first. That is the tallit. The next item of religious garb is the *tefillin*.

Tefillin: What Are They?

Tefillin (Heb., *prayer*) or *phylacteries* (Gr., *amulet*) consist of two small black leather boxes. Attached to these one- to two-inch cubes are long leather straps two to three feet in length. One of the boxes is placed on the forehead (*shel rosh*), and the other is placed on the arm (*shel yad*).

The shel yad contains passages of Scripture written by a scribe on one piece of parchment. These passages, taken from the Torah, are Exodus 13:1-16, and Deuteronomy 6:4-9; 11:13-21.

The shel rosh contains the same Scriptures, but they are written on four separate pieces of parchment, the Exodus portion being divided between verses 10 and 11. Each tiny parchment is inserted into one of four separate compartments in the cube.

Tefillin: Why Are They Worn?

Interpreting these Torah passages literally, the rabbis of old fashioned the tefillin to comply with the command to make them "a token upon thine hand, and for frontlets between thine eyes" (Exodus 13:16). Symbolically, they are to remind worshipers of their commitment and consecration to the God who redeemed His people after four centuries of bondage in Egypt. They are also a reminder that God owns the worshiper's heart and intellect. For this reason, shel yad points to the heart, and shel rosh is worn on the head.

Originally worn all day long as a constant display of commitment, tefillin were outlawed in ancient Rome. Today they are donned as part of the morning worship, either at home or in the synagogue.

Tefillin: How Do You Put Them On?

The shel yad is placed just above the elbow with the box pointed toward the heart, always on the weaker arm. Thus, if a person is right-handed, the cube is placed on the left arm, and vice versa. This rule comes from a rabbinic interpretation of Deuteronomy 6:8-9, which teaches that the hand that writes should be the hand that binds.

The leather strap is wrapped around the arm seven times. This practice is based on the seven Hebrew words in Psalm 145:16, "Thou openest thine hand, and satisfiest the desire of every living thing." Ashkenazic (eastern European ancestry) Jews wrap the strap clockwise; Sephardic (Mediterranean ancestry) Jews wrap it counterclockwise. The strap is then wound three times around the ring and middle fingers, forming the Hebrew letter for *Shaddai*, meaning *Almighty*. The three windings recall the passage in Hosea 2:19-20, which contains God's three-fold commitment to Israel: "I will betroth thee unto me forever; yea, I will betroth thee unto me in righteousness....I will even betroth thee unto me in faithfulness."

As the worshipers begins their daily ritual, they recite the following blessing in Hebrew: "Praised be thou, O Lord our God, King of the universe, who has sanctified us through His commandments and commanded us to wear tefillin." The shel rosh is then placed on the forehead between the eyes, just below the hairline. A special knot is made to secure the tefila (singular) on the head. A blessing—"Praised be Thou, O Lord our God, King of the universe, who has sanctified us with His commandments and commanded us concerning the law of tefillin"—is then recited.

Zeal is an attribute that has never been found wanting in Judaism. Indeed, those who adhere to its many traditions do not lack courage or conviction, and Christians can learn a great deal from them. Yet a built-in problem arises whenever the traditions themselves replace the reasons for them. Matthew 23:5 records that flaw as stated by the Lord Himself: "But all their works they do to be seen of men; they make broad their phylacteries, and enlarge the borders of their garments" (tallit).

The writer to the Hebrews wrote, "But we see Jesus" (Hebrews 2:9). Believers are admonished not to dress with outward adornments but to "put...on the Lord Jesus Christ" (Romans 13:14) daily.

A JEW LIVES HERE

Jewish people who are serious about practicing their Judaism realize that living incognito is not an option for them. Judaism, by its very nature, teaches its people not to be ashamed of their identity. Jewish practice, by its very essence, forces a distinction from neighboring Gentiles. This distinction can be seen clearly by observing Jewish diet, dress, and worship. Consistent with this is the God-given command to display publicly God's Word: "And thou shalt write them upon the posts of thy house, and on thy gates" (Deuteronomy 6:9). Jewish people have taken this commandment literally, displaying these words for two reasons. First, they serve as a reminder of the individual privileges and responsibilities each Jew has before the living God. Second, they serve to mark out a Jewish home, letting the community know that *a Jew lives there*.

The name of this distinguishing mark is *mezuza* (pronounced meh-ZOO-zah), which means *doorpost.* Mezuzas (the Hebrew plural is *mezuzot*) are small oblong boxes made of various materials—often wood or some type of metal, and these days even glass or acrylic. They hold two small portions of God's Word, Deuteronomy 6:4-9 and Deuteronomy 11:13-21. These verses are penned onto a small piece of parchment (*klaf*) by a scribe, rolled up, and placed inside the container. According to Jewish law, a mezuza must be placed on the lintel of every doorway in the house, except the bathrooms.

Each mezuza must have the name *Shaddai* on the front. This can be accomplished either by placing a hole in the case so that the word is displayed from the carefully rolled-up parchment, or by writing the word on the case itself. Shaddai is one of the many names of God recorded in the Jewish Scriptures. It means *almighty* or *sufficient.* Eight times it appears to communicate the truth that God is all-sufficient and almighty. Jewish interpreters believe that three Hebrew letters—*Shin, Daled,* and *Yud*—are an acronym of the phrase *shomer delet Israel* (*guardian of the door of Israel*).

Several points must be considered regarding Jewish law and the mezuza. First, it must contain real parchment made from the skin of a kosher animal. Second, a scribe must pen the verses onto the parchment. Third, before the mezuza is placed on the doorpost, a blessing must be recited: "Blessed art Thou, Lord our God, King of the universe, Who has sanctified us with His commandments and commanded us to affix mezuza." Fourth, the mezuza must be affixed with nails, screws, or glue to the right side of the door. It must be placed about a third of the way from the top of the doorpost. Fifth, the mezuza must be tilted 45 degrees at an inward angle—that is, toward the house. Sixth, the parchment must be removed every few years to make sure that it is in good condition.

Perhaps you have seen Jewish people put their fingers to the mezuza and then to their lips as they enter or leave a room. It is customary to touch the mezuza and then kiss the fingers as a demonstration of respect, love, and devotion to God and to His commandments.

It is not uncommon to see mezuzas in places other than the doorpost. Some people wear small mezuzas around their necks as necklaces or as charms on bracelets. When I was growing up, my parents had a magnetic mezuza mounted on the dashboard of our car. These uses are permissible, as long as they are intended as symbols of the owner's identification with the Jewish people. However, the mezuza should not be used as a talisman or a lucky charm; to use it in this way is considered unworthy.

A familiar Jewish story is told of a very religious man whose children sent him on a nice vacation. The man was hesitant to go because he was concerned that the hotel might not be kosher, although his children assured him that it was. They knew he would never stay in a place that did not meet the standards of Jewish law. When the man arrived, the manager gladly escorted him around the building, making it a point to stop at the kitchen. The manager wanted his guest to see for himself that everything was strictly kosher. Later, when they arrived at the room where the elderly man would be staying, he reached up his hand to touch the mezuza. Much to his surprise, there was no mezuza! "Where is the mezuza?" shrieked the old man. "Not to worry," the manager calmly replied. "This hotel is equipped with a master mezuza that we keep on the roof."

From time to time in my travels, I have visited the homes of Gentile believers who have placed mezuzas in their entryways. Why would believers, redeemed by the one who fulfilled the law, display mezuzas? Here are some of the reasons given to me: "I love the Jewish people." "I want to identify myself with the Jewish people." "It is a reminder for me to pray for them." "It serves as a reminder of God's relationship with His Chosen People and His relationship with me."

One thing seems clear. We, as Christian believers, can glean this truth from the mezuza. We may not need an outward, tangible sign, but our attitude and practice should convey clearly to those around us that *a Christian lives here.*

SIDDUR: THE BOOK OF PRAYER

Like so many other Jewish adults, I well remember the long and arduous process of learning the liturgy of Hebrew prayers involved in worship. It started with the simple rote learning of the Hebrew alphabet. Once our teacher was convinced that we had mastered the Hebrew letters, he taught us to say and understand vocabulary until we became proficient readers. Next came the introduction to a thick, intimidating book, bound in white leather, called the *Siddur.* It was exciting to realize that we were communicating with the Creator in the language of heaven, as we had been taught it was. The Siddur contains most, if not all, of the prayers to be recited in a Jewish person's life. For this reason, the Jewish community places a high value on familiarity with this most holy book. The distinctiveness of Jewish prayer can be seen through a cursory examination of the Siddur, the *book of prayer.*

In the table of contents of a Siddur you will immediately see the reason for its name. *Siddur* means *order,* and in this case it is the order of prayers. It is, however, much more than a prayer book, for inherent in the various prayers are a conglomerate of biblical, talmudic, and rabbinical regulations. The Siddur, by its very nature, is a source of unity in Judaism, a religion whose adherents otherwise differ greatly in their beliefs and opinions. Visit any synagogue around the world and you will find essentially the same prayer book, for its contents are a universal entity among Jewish people.

The types and times of prayer are designated by the Siddur. Three types of prayers are found. The first type is *Praise*, which is designed to praise God as the Creator of the heavens and the earth. A praise prayer always involves the declaration of God's holiness, kindness, goodness, and power, as well as extolling His very name. A second type of prayer is *Thanksgiving*. This is simply a recognition of the fact that God has poured out abundant blessings upon His people. These prayers express thanks to God for the Torah (God's Word), as well as appreciation for our heritage, history, and the supply of our daily provision. The third type of prayer is *Supplication*. This is how most people view prayer—asking God to meet a need. While this is a definite part of Jewish prayer, it is by no means the part most emphasized. Most of the requests are national in scope, rather than personal. Requests such as peace for the world, a desire for the Messiah to come, and a desire for the Temple to be rebuilt are but a few of the suppliant prayers in the Siddur. On a more personal level, there are prayers for a prosperous and healthy life and for all men to live like brothers.

Once we understand the types of Jewish prayer, we must learn the times when they are to be prayed. Daily prayers are recited every morning (*Shacharit*), noon (*Mincha*), and evening (*Ma'ariv*). This practice undoubtedly came from the example of

Daniel, who prayed three times a day, as recorded in Daniel 6:10. The psalmist wrote, "Evening, and morning, and at noon, will I pray, and cry aloud, and he shall hear my voice" (Psalm 55:17). According to the Talmud, Abraham instituted the morning prayer, Isaac the afternoon prayer, and Jacob the evening prayer.

Shacharit is the longest of the three daily times of prayer. It represents the early morning sacrifice brought to the Temple and must take place between sunrise and noon. Included in it are various blessings and songs, as well as prayers for the Monday, Thursday, and Sabbath readings of the Torah. One prayer is common to all three times of daily prayer—the *Shemoneh Esrei*, which means *18 blessings*. Because the worshiper stands to recite this prayer, it is also known as the *Amida* (*standing*). Interestingly, a 19th blessing was added over the course of time, but the name remains Shemoneh Esrei. It is also at the morning service that the tefillin, or phylacteries, are worn.

Mincha takes place in the afternoon, after one o'clock and before sunset. It is the shortest of the daily prayers, yet it is considered the most rewarding because it is difficult to take time out of a business day to recite its liturgy. Thus, the "sacrifice" should deserve a reward. Three prayers are recited, including the Shemoneh Esrei; the happy prayer called *Ashrei*, which is Psalm 145; and *Aleinu*, which proclaims God as King over all humanity. Ma'ariv, the evening service, can be prayed any time after sunset and before sunrise. Included in this service are the *Shema* (Deuteronomy 6:4), Shemoneh Esrei, and Aleinu.

Other prayer times are listed in the Siddur. One is for the Sabbath, which, in addition to the other daily prayers, includes some prayers that are unique for this day of rest. There are also prayers for the many holy days and festivals.

Certainly one of the most difficult times in life is when a loved one passes on. It is at this time that the *Kaddish* (*sanctification*) is recited. Often thought to be a prayer for the dead, it actually is an Aramaic poem that wonderfully exalts God's name. The Kaddish is patterned after Job 13:15, which states, "Though he slay me, yet will I trust him." It has no direct reference to God. The Kaddish is a prayer that almost every Jew will recognize:

> Hallowed and enhanced may He be throughout the world of His own creation....May He be praised throughout all time....Glorified and celebrated, lauded and praised, acclaimed and honored, extolled and exalted....May the prayers and pleas of the whole house of Israel be accepted by our Father in Heaven.

The last section of the Siddur contains prayers to be recited before and after meals, weddings, births, circumcisions, and times of illness. Thus, the entire range of human life is covered by these prescribed prayers.

Speaking from experience, as well as observation, I must say, sadly, that the weakness of the prayers in the Siddur is not in the content of the prayers, but rather in the lack of understanding on the part of those praying them. The inherent beauty and sincerity are lost.

Those of us who believe that Jesus is our Messiah can pray from a book or from the heart without learning a special language. Our emphasis should be to "Pray without ceasing" (1 Thessalonians 5:17) and, like our Jewish friends, to be in awe of the privilege of personal communication with the Creator of the universe.

THE DYNAMIC OF JEWISH PRAYER

Am I a God at hand, saith the LORD, and not a God afar off? Can any hide himself in secret places that I shall not see him? saith the LORD. Do not I fill heaven and earth? saith the LORD (Jeremiah 23:23-24).

Many principles guide Jewish prayer, but none is more concise than God's revelation through His prophet. The dynamic of Jewish prayer hinges on a comprehension of the awesome attributes of the God of Israel. The previous section in this chapter—on the Siddur—related the times of and, to some extent, content of various daily prayers. This section on prayer gives insight into Judaism's place for the little, seemingly insignificant aspects of daily life. Things that may be taken for granted by others are seriously addressed in Judaism, directing the followers to be aware at all times that God has a role in all that they do. From the time they awake in the morning until their heads hit the pillow at night, Jewish people recite prayers that point to distinctives about God.

Preparation for the worship of God comes about almost immediately upon rising in the morning. The priests who ministered in and around the Temple purified themselves by washing before their service; therefore, each Jew must ritually spill water three times. Not only does this physically cleanse the hands, but it symbolizes the removal of all impurities as spiritual purity is restored. A full cup of water is placed in the left hand and spilled into the right. Then another full cup of water is spilled from the right hand into the left. This is done three times. Upon completion of this ritual, a blessing is recited: "Blessed art Thou, O Lord our God, King of the universe, who sanctified us with His commandments and commanded us con-

cerning the washing of hands." It is noteworthy that the usual
Hebrew word for *hands* is not used in this prayer. Instead, the
word used here implies *lifted hands*. Thus, the idea of consecration to God starts immediately upon awaking in the morning.
The rabbis say that no one should walk around without first
washing the hands in this manner.

Once this cleansing is completed and before any other
necessary activity—eating, working, transacting business, or
beginning a journey—prayer must take place. The worshipers must have their bodies cleansed and adorned with
clean clothes, and they must be placed in a spot that is clean
as well. Amos the prophet said it well: "Prepare to meet thy
God" (Amos 4:12). The worshipers pray a prayer thanking
God for keeping them alive through the night, acknowledging that without Him, "it would be impossible to survive and
to stand before Thee."

Unlike Christians, who believe that human beings are
born sinful, Judaism teaches that, "As God is pure, so is
man's soul pure." As a result of that teaching, a prayer of
thanksgiving is offered to God for restoring the soul from
sleep. A number of Talmudic prayers, all beginning with
"Blessed art Thou, O Lord our God, King of the universe..."
are recited, such as "who opens the eyes of the blind," "who
clothes the naked," "who releases the bound," "who sets
forth the earth upon the waters," "who girds Israel with
might," "who crowns Israel with glory," and "who gives
strength to the weary." One of the final prayers recited soon
after arising encourages the worshipers to implore God to
"Lead us not into sin or transgression and iniquity, or into
temptation or disgrace; let not the impulse toward evil rule
over us....Give us this day and every day grace, favor, and
mercy—in thy sight and in the sight of all men." These and

other prayers affirm that God should be remembered and praised for all things.

Two controversial daily prayers of thanks have as their heading, "Who has not made me...." It is easy to see why they are controversial. The first expresses thanksgiving to God for not being made a Gentile, while the second gives thanks for not being made a woman. The explanation for these Talmudic prayers is simple, although not convincing to many people. Both are recited because of the tremendous privileges in keeping the commandments of God. Gentiles do not have to keep the commandments because they are not the Chosen People. Women—Jewish women—are responsible for taking care of the family and home and thus are not obligated to follow the commandments.

Part of everyday living involves eating. Individual prayers are recited for various foods and are chanted before eating. However, the Torah says, "When thou hast eaten and art full, then thou shalt bless the LORD thy God for the good land which he hath given thee" (Deuteronomy 8:10). This command is fulfilled by reciting a series of blessings: *Birkat Hazan*—for the food that sustains life; *Birkat Haaretz*—for the land given to the Jewish people by God; and *Birkat Yerushalayim*—for Jerusalem, that restoration of Temple worship and the King will return. A fourth blessing, *Birkat Hatov V'hametiv*, has been added to communicate God's goodness. All four are recited when the meal is over.

Self-evaluation at the end of the day is extremely important. This inventory of deeds is to be done before the Shema (Deuteronomy 4:6) is recited. There must be "remorse, repentance and whole-hearted resolve not to repeat the transgression." Also, forgiveness must be granted for any wrong committed against a person on that day.

Upon completion of prayers, a universal word—*Amen*—is used to pronounce a strong endorsement. This word appears 23 times in the Jewish Scriptures, most notably in Deuteronomy 27:16-26. One rabbi stresses that the three Hebrew letters in Amen stand for *God*, *Faithful*, and *King*, thus solidifying the importance of that biblical word. When Jewish people hear a blessing, whether pronounced by a Jew or a Gentile, the law states that they must say, "Amen."

It is clear that those who love the Savior—the Messiah of Israel—can benefit greatly from an understanding of the absolute obedience and commitment that daily Jewish prayer demands. Jewish prayer is designed to prevent the worshipers from taking God for granted. This reverence for the Holy One of Israel should be an area of common ground that we, as believers, share with our observant Jewish friends.

PRAYER: THE SERVICE OF THE HEART

Prayer is not unique to Judaism, yet Jewish prayer is unique. In synagogues around the world, congregants meet together to worship. But Jewish prayer is not confined to a synagogue. On a flight to the Holy Land, it is not uncommon to see Orthodox Jewish men gathering in the back of a 747 as the sun rises in the east, wearing prayer shawls and carrying siddurs in their hands, much to the amazement of their fellow travelers. As they open their bags of religious paraphernalia, they begin to chant softly and sway gently. At the Western or Wailing Wall in Jerusalem, Jewish prayer can be seen graphically as worshipers recite various prayers, often with great emotion. And what pilgrim to the promised land has not been moved to write a special prayer and insert in into the cracks of the Wall's huge stones?

Whether in a synagogue, on board a 747, at the Wall, or in private homes, prayer holds a central place for the Jewish people.

Jewish Prayer: Introduced in the Old Testament —

The English word *pray* is defined by such words as *implore, entreat,* or even *beg.* Most people think of the word as asking or petitioning God. The Hebrew word *L'hitpalel* carries no such idea. At its root is the word *pll,* which means *to judge.* Thus, regardless of the kind of prayer, when people pray, they are, in a real sense, judging themselves as they interact with God.

Jewish Scripture gives numerous examples of individuals crying out, seeking, and inquiring of God in prayer. The Psalmist stated it well when he said, "The LORD is near unto all those who call upon him, to all who call upon him in truth" (Palm 145:18). It seems clear that the prayers of the Old Testament Hebrew were simple, spontaneous, and self-less. In addition, these prayers were almost always group-conscious and "other"-centered. The prayer offered by Solomon at the dedication of the Temple contains four elements of Hebrew prayer: thanksgiving, praise, confession, and intercession. Formal prescribed prayers, even commanded prayers, were not part of Jewish prayer until the time of the second Temple.

Jewish Prayer: Interpreted by the Rabbis —

Using Deuteronomy 11:13, the rabbis determined that prayer holds a supreme position in Jewish thought, calling it "the service of the heart." After Herod's Temple was destroyed, prayer was regarded as a substitute for the sacrifices. Later it came to be considered a means to forgive sin.

Jewish prayer is distinct in several ways. First, it is spoken in Hebrew, a practice preferred although not prescribed. This being the case, the more Orthodox the congregation, the more Hebrew is used in its prayers. Many find this practice frustrating, either because they are unable to read the Hebrew words or because they read the words without understanding what they are saying. However, this practice is defended in the following ways.

1. Hebrew is the language of the Torah, the "sacred tongue," and as such unites Jews as a people.

2. The use of Hebrew ensures that Jewish people will feel reasonably at home in their synagogues.

3. The use of Hebrew serves as a means of binding the people with the land of Israel.

4. The use of Hebrew checks the possibility of total assimilation into a non-Jewish culture.

The second distinctive of Jewish prayer is its fixed liturgy. One rabbi comments that "liturgy unites, theology divides." It is believed that the use of siddurim (prayer books) affords worshipers the opportunity to think of things about God that they may not have thought of on their own. In addition, liturgy instills a sense of community as prayers are recited together to God.

The third distinctive of Jewish prayer is that a minimum number of ten men is required to pray corporately. This quorum is called a minyan. The practice is taken from the Torah (Numbers 14). There the ten spies were considered a congregation. While private prayer is allowed, it is regarded as a special mitzvah (good deed) to pray as part of a congregation. The importance of corporate prayer can be seen clearly in the rabbinical teaching that if you cannot be pre-

sent for corporate prayer, you can at least schedule your private prayers to coincide with those of the congregation. This
aspect of Jewish prayer is yet another way to remind Jews
that they are a social people who can be encouraged by being
around one another.

Jewish Prayer: Intensity of the Heart ———

Central to the concept of Jewish prayer is *kavanah*, the devotion that the rabbis direct to God during prayer. It is concentration; it is sincerity; it is praying as though the *shekinah* (*glory* of
God) is present. Kavanah is a quiet calm and an assurance as people recite the prayers. Maimonides said, "Prayer without devotion is not prayer....He whose thoughts are wandering or occupied with other things ought not to pray...before engaging in
prayer the worshiper ought to bring himself into a devotional
frame of mind."

As we have looked at some of the issues of Jewish prayer, we
may want to examine our own state of mind as we approach our
Father in heaven. May we be unencumbered by wandering
thoughts, having our minds set on Him.

TZEDAKA: IT IS MORE BLESSED TO GIVE

A story is told of the rabbi of Nemirov. His followers,
all Hasidim, stated emphatically that every night their rabbi
went up to heaven. Another Jewish group, *Mitnaggedim*
(*opponents*), ridiculed the Hasidim about this belief. One
particular Mitnagged thought the idea so preposterous that
one night he decided to hide under the rabbi's bed to con-
firm firsthand the impossibility of such a thing. At about 2
a.m., the rabbi arose, put on his coat, and took an ax in his
hand. The frightened but well-hidden doubter followed the

rabbi into the forest. Keeping his distance, he watched as the rabbi began to chop down trees then cut the wood into logs suitable for burning. He marveled as he saw the rabbi deliver his secret offering to the widows and the infirm in the town. The next morning in synagogue, when the Hasidim spoke of their rabbi going to heaven, the former nonbeliever surprised his group of followers and said, "Yes—to heaven, if not even higher."

This wonderful but little-known story eloquently captures the essence of the Jewish idea of charity or giving. Because there is no literal Hebrew word for charity, the word *tzedaka* (pronounced tse-DOCK-a), meaning *righteousness*, is used. Synonyms for *tzedaka* are *justice, truth,* and *kindness,* making clear the importance of the redeeming qualities of giving within Judaism.

The Bible has much to say about giving. Numbers 7 alone devotes all of its 89 verses, almost 2,000 words, to giving. The Torah contains a variety of laws applying to the poor. Tithes for the poor (*ma'aser ani*), the gleaning of the field (*leket*), the year of release (*shemittah*), and the field corner to be reaped by the poor (*peah*) all relate to the Jewish idea of giving as justice. At the same time, compassion is also an integral part of giving. Deuteronomy 15:7-11 states that because there would always be poor people in the land of Israel, the Israelites were to stretch their hands out wide to those poor brethren around them and give without evil in their hearts. Proverbs 19:17 says that giving to the poor is like lending to the Lord.

Maimonides made a list of different kinds of contributions to charity. From the least kind of giving to the greatest kind of giving, his ranking reads:

8. He who doesn't give enough and even that unwillingly, and in bad grace.

7. He who doesn't give enough (according to his means) but what he does give he donates with good grace.

6. He who gives after he is asked.

5. He who gives before he is asked (both parties knowing each other).

4. He who "casts among the poor," meaning that the recipient knows who gave, but the donor doesn't know who received.

3. He who knows who is to get the money but sees to it that this person does not learn who gave it and thus avoids any embarrassment on his part.

2. He who gives charity without knowing who is to receive it and without the recipient being told who gave it.

1. He who helps someone save his business or get a job so that it will not become necessary for this person to become dependent on charity.

Other examples of the place charity holds in Jewish literature abound:

- Charity equals all the other commandments.

- A penny for the poor will obtain a view of the Shekinah.

- Whom God loves He sends a golden opportunity for charity.

- By benevolence man rises to a height where he meets God.

- What you give to charity in health is gold, what you give in sickness is silver, and what you give after death is copper.

Other well-used statements on giving in Judaism are:

- For your purposes it is more important to give often than to give much.

- When you remember yourself, be sure to remember others.

- One never asks questions when people want food, even if they are complete strangers.

It seems evident that, biblically and talmudically, giving is an integral part of Jewish life. Therefore, it is not surprising that Jewish people are very generous. They are key players in the leadership of charitable organizations, especially those involving education (religious and secular), health care, and the arts. To what can we attribute this generosity? An old Yiddish proverb states, "The longest road in the world is the one that leads from your pocketbook." Understanding the truth behind the humor in that adage, Judaism begins teaching about giving while its people are very young. As a child, I was taught various ways of giving, most of which centered around the synagogue. Funds for Israel, education, and immigration were usually raised by pledges. An old but effective way of developing habitual giving involved something called a *pushke*, which is a small collection box kept in the home. Various charitable groups will supply the pushke, have the family keep it for a period of time (usually a week), and pick it up before the Sabbath. Families collect money for any number of charities—trees for Israel, homes for senior citizens, widows, various brotherhoods, sponsoring passage to Israel for those who wish to migrate but cannot afford it, buying food for the hungry, etc.

We can learn much from observing our Jewish friends in the area of giving. Scripturally based, Judaism demonstrates that intertwined with its relationship to the Almighty is a compassionate and heartfelt eye on those of humble means. Our family has adopted the use of a pushke to collect money for various causes. We sit down together and talk about where we want to contribute this money.

Christianity, which was born from Judaism, differs, not in the importance of giving, but in the motivation to give. Nothing we do can make us righteous, but the Messiah's followers will give and do so joyously because they have been given the greatest gift of all—salvation!

ENDNOTES

[1] Donin, Rabbi Hayim Halevy, *To Be a Jew* (New York: Basic Books, Inc., 1972), p. 164.

[2] *Encyclopaedia Judaica*, "Reading of Shema" (New York: Macmillan Company, 1971), pp. 1370-1374.

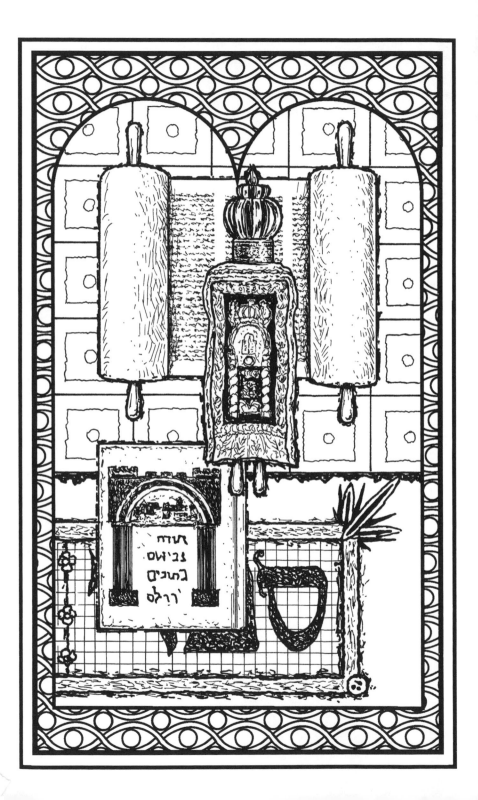

JEWISH LITERATURE

TENACH, TORAH, AND TARGUM

The Torah is the foundation stone for the Jewish people. Inspired by God and written by Moses, it has been central to Jewish life since its inception. The desire to read and understand the Word of God is biblical, established at a time in Jewish history when the people were aware of their need to get back to the basics of their faith. Nehemiah 8:1-8 records that the people were gathered together as Ezra the scribe brought out the book of the Law of Moses. He then faced the street, standing before the Water Gate, and read aloud from morning until midday, as the people stood listening. Nehemiah made it a point to explain that the priests caused the people to understand.

That event, which took place some 2,400 years ago, demonstrated a desire to know God and understand His Word.

The Jewish people of that day, however, would find it difficult
to identify with their contemporaries of the 20th century.
Jewish literature has had a profound effect on its people regarding the practices and beliefs of their faith. Alfred Kolatch put
it well when he said (speaking of a Jew in Solomon's or Moses'
day), "Our visitor from the past would have to learn that the
laws of the Bible, although primary and central, are not the
only source of Jewish practice."

This chapter will examine the literature that has so affected
the Jewish people. Starting with the Torah and branching
beyond, we will survey various writings and the effects they have
had on the Jewish people.

When referring to the Holy Scriptures, the Jewish people
do not think in terms of Testaments. The Bible or *Tenach* is
divided into three divisions. The *Torah* or *Law* is made up of
Genesis, Exodus, Leviticus, Numbers, and Deuteronomy.
The *Nebi'im* or *Prophets* is comprised of the historical books
of Joshua, Judges, 1 and 2 Samuel, 1 and 2 Kings, the major
prophets Isaiah, Jeremiah, and Ezekiel, and the minor
prophets Hosea, Joel, Amos, Obadiah, Jonah, Micah,
Nahum, Habakkuk, Zephaniah, Haggai, Zechariah, and
Malachi. The *Kethubim* or *Writings* are divided into the
Wisdom Books of Psalms, Proverbs, and Job and the *Megiloth*,
consisting of Song of Songs, Ruth, Lamentations,
Ecclesiastes, and Esther. Also included in the Kethubim are
the prophets Ezra, Nehemiah, and Daniel and the history
books of 1 and 2 Chronicles. The word *Tenach* is formed
from an acrostic, using the first letter of each of the three
divisions, *T-N-CH*, to signify the whole Bible.

The Torah is held in high esteem for two reasons. First,
the author is God, sometimes referred to as the "King of the
Universe." Second, the content covers the topics that are

most relevant to everyday practical living—family, civil law, and theology.

The word *Torah* means *teaching* or *doctrine*. There is a tradition that the Torah was in existence in heaven and was merely brought down to Moses at Mount Sinai. It may be this belief that causes some to consider the Torah more authoritative than the other two parts of the Jewish Scriptures. Another tradition holds that God offered the Torah to all the nations of the world, but all refused it except Israel.

The Old Testament, as we know it, contains 39 books, yet the Jewish Scriptures have been arranged into 24 books. The 12 minor prophets are counted as one book, and the books of 1 and 2 Samuel, 1 and 2 Kings, and 1 and 2 Chronicles are each considered one book.

The title or word *Torah* has been broadened and, at least in conversation, has lost its technical meaning. If people are reading or studying Torah, they are most likely going beyond the five books of Moses. In this context, they are probably studying not only the three divisions in the Scriptures, but commentaries and other extra-biblical texts as well.

The prophets are read in the synagogue on the Sabbath and holidays. This portion of Scripture is read by young men and women at their bar/bat mitzvahs. In the technical sense, all Jewish Scriptures are equal; yet it is not uncommon for some to regard the five books of Moses as more authoritative than the other two sections.

The Writings have been a source of encouragement for God's chosen people for millennia. Read during the various feasts and looked to during times of difficulty, they have brought strength and hope through the philosophy, poetry, and proverbs they offer.

The word *canon* means *measuring rod* and is used to describe the standard by which books were considered biblical. The original language of the Bible is predominately Hebrew, along with a little Aramaic. At the time of Ezra and Nehemiah, most Jewish people did not speak Hebrew, so the few who could read and speak both languages communicated the Word of God to the people in the Aramaic language. These teachers or scribes became known as interpreters. As the Hebrew text was translated, the resulting treatise was referred to as the *Targum.* Not all of these translations were literal; some were paraphrases and others were interpreted along with stories supplied by the translators.

Another group of teachers, the *Sopherim* or *scribes,* had the task of copying the Holy Scriptures. In addition, they committed themselves to public instruction. They became known collectively as the Great Assembly, and from this group the Sanhedrin later arose.

Extremely important is the tradition that more than the written Torah exists. The Oral Law is believed to have come from God's mouth to Moses on Mount Sinai. He, in turn, passed it on to Joshua, who handed it down to the elders, who gave it to the prophets, who entrusted it to the Great Assembly. The Oral Law was memorized in its entirety by each generation, until it was finally written down. It is this other law, coupled with the input of the various teachers along the way, that complicates a deeper understanding of Jewish literature.

Many of us are familiar with the saying, "God said it, I believe it, and that settles it." While many Jewish people would say "Amen" to that sentiment, a problem ensues when Jewish men of renown debate *who* said it and *who* believes it.

THE TALMUD

"No! No! No!" the grandmother screamed as the six-year-old boy placed the clean spoon into the drawer of clean utensils. "That spoon goes with the *Milchig* [*dairy*]." The youngster should have known; it was one of the rules he had learned early in life. But remembering that dairy products and everything they touch must remain separate from meat and everything associated with it (including clean dishes and utensils) was not always easy, despite his grandmother's startling reminder. That event from many years ago is still etched in my memory. I was that boy. Our family's eating habits were governed by the rabbinical interpretation of the biblical law, "Thou shalt not boil a kid in his mother's milk" (Exodus 23:19).

The lifestyle of millions of Jewish families has been formed, shaped, and developed over the years by rabbinical interpretation, commentary, regulation, and homilies of the Jewish Scripture. After hundreds of years of memorizing the increasing wisdom and knowledge of what was called the Oral Law, the great Jewish academies of Jerusalem and Babylon forged an incredible compilation and systematic work that would serve as a kind of encyclopedia of rabbinical commentary. It is called the *Talmud*.

As the basic text and primary source for Jewish law, the Talmud, which means *teaching, studying,* or *process of learning*, covers almost every conceivable area of human interest. Actually there are two Talmuds. One is called the *Palestinian* or *Jerusalem Talmud* (*Yerushalim*), after its place of origin, and the other is called *Babylonian* (*Babli*), also after its place of origin, Babylon. Contributors to the Palestinian Talmud, which was completed in 350 A.D., lived in such Israeli cities as Tiberias, Safad, and Caesarea. The Babylonian Talmud, containing well over two million words, is about three times the size of the Palestinian Talmud. Its contributors lived in such Babylonian cities as Sura, Nahardea, and Pumbeditha. It was finished in 500 A.D. Of the two, it is regarded as the more authoritative.

The Talmud is divided into two sections, the *Mishna* (*repeat*) and *Gemora* (*supplements*). The Mishna is a vast, divergent commentary on the Scriptures from sages and scholars before 220 A.D. It was compiled and edited by Judah Hanasi (the Prince), the great-grandson of the famous Hillel, from the great sages called *Tannaim*. The Gemora, written in Aramaic, is a *completion* of opinions, illustrations, and decisions of scholars called *Amoraim*. Simply stated, it is a commentary on the commentary.

The Mishna is divided into six orders, each order having a number of *tractates* or *sections* (63 in all). The orders are as follows: *Zeraim* (*seeds*)—eleven tractates, all relating to laws concerning agriculture, crops, and gifts for the poor; *Moed* (*festivals*)—twelve tractates dealing with feasts, fast days, and Sabbath laws; *Nashim* (*women*)—seven tractates expounding on laws relating to marriage, as well as rulings on incest, divorce, and property; *Nezikin* (*damages*)—ten tractates devoted to civil and penal laws, vows, punishments, etc.; *Kodeshim* (*holy things*)—eleven tractates addressing the laws of the Temple and sacrifices; and *Toharot* (*purity*)—twelve tractates stating the laws of ritual purity. The Talmud combines the two writings. Thus, you may have three or four lines of Mishna written in Hebrew, followed by several pages of Gemora written in Aramaic.

The Talmud contains two distinct types of material: *Halacha*, meaning *to follow*, which covers the laws and observances of the Jewish people; and *Aggadah*, meaning *narration*, which covers personal, social, national, and international relationships.

Once the Talmud was completed, it became apparent that scholars were having trouble understanding what was written. Although it was arranged into subject matter, the contents of the Talmud are not arranged logically, and the material becomes very technical. In addition, there are numerous abbreviations, foreign words, and difficult idioms. In light of this situation, many rabbis and scholars over the years have devoted themselves to providing "helps," such as dictionaries and lexicons, guides, and codes to help in understanding the Talmud. Eventually some of these "helps" found themselves within the pages of the Talmud for easy reference.

Over the years, the study of the Talmud has been limited. The early copies were all handwritten and were thus difficult to secure, even to copy. The first known printed copy was completed in Guadalajara, Spain, in 1482. Remnants of that work still survive.

Another difficulty was the prohibition to study the Talmud imposed by so-called "Christians" (not born-again believers, as we know them). The "church" was having difficulty with the trend of rationalistic thinking. Part of the method of suppressing independent thinking of its members was to foster a "clergy only" interpretation. The Talmud posed a real threat to that philosophy because of the various rabbis commenting on Scripture. Several popes ordered Talmuds confiscated and burned in Rome, France, and Poland.

Today, access to the Talmud is as easy as a walk through the bookstore at the local mall or even punching it up on a CD-ROM for your computer. Most Jewish people around the world have the freedom to study it, but only a small percentage take advantage of that freedom.

It cannot be emphasized enough that, while rabbinical insight can be helpful, the view that the Talmud is equal to Scripture is false. If only my grandmother had understood that, she might not have been so upset over the misplaced silverware!

KABBALAH:
MAKING A MYSTERY OF GOD'S WORD

An expert is defined as a person who displays a special knowledge derived from training or experience. More than two decades ago, as a junior in college, I was boarding with several other students—all Gentiles. In that environment, I regarded myself as an expert on Jewish things, calling on my years of living in a religiously observant home to answer any philosophic or religious inquiries they might have. My bubble was burst, however, when I found one of my roommates poring over Jewish-looking books. As we talked, I learned that he was pursuing a personal study of *Kabbalah*. Other than a familiarity with the term, I knew very little about it. I asked him two questions: "What is it? And why would you (or anyone else) want to study it?"

Kabbalah (*received by tradition*) is a vast collection of biblical writings heavily augmented with superstition, astrology, spiritism, and mystical thinking. At first, this knowledge was limited to a few selected (according to Jewish belief, from heaven) people. It was propelled to prominence during the suffering and persecution experienced by Jewish people in the Middle Ages.

To the Kabbalist, every word is divine, and every letter in the Hebrew alphabet is full of power. Its message is simple enough for a youngster but filled with hidden messages that can take the Kabbalist to great spiritual depth and power. Unlocking these hidden messages demands further study in numerology, Gnostic thought, and dualistic thinking. With these occultic tools, the Kabbalist is guided by two overriding principles. The first is redemption for suffering through a pursuit of the knowledge of God. The second is a pursuit of righteousness and spiritual purity to bring in the Messiah. Various topics are investigated: the essence of the Supreme Being, the universe and its beginning, the creation of mankind and its destiny, and angels and their destiny. The Kabbalist's desire is to master the "spiritual highway" the same way personalities such as Moses, Elijah, Elisha, and Ezekiel were believed to have done.

In Kabbalistic thinking, God is viewed as infinite, endless, and boundless; He is called the *Ain Soph*. Humans, as finite creatures, are capable of comprehending or relating to the Ain Soph only through prayer, meditation, and a willingness to be spiritual receptacles. Thus, they learn the power of the ten *Sephiroth*, the energies that emanate from the Soph to form the universe. These energies are associated with aspects of the human being: the world of thought, the world of the soul, and the world of the body. If this sounds a bit complex, brace yourself—these are but the basics. This universe of ten spheres, when united, could be broken down into four worlds: action (the lowest), formation (next highest), creation (next highest), and emanations (the highest).

Through Kabbalah, people can project themselves into another world, a world different from the world of the Talmudist, which is made up of the objective and the rational. This mystical world has incredible potential for spiritual advancement. It is a most appealing world to those repeatedly subjected to anti-Semitism.

Kabbalistic doctrine has explanations for many biblical doctrines. Hell, for instance, is not an external place of suffering but a suffering from within. Satan is an evil being, created by God to minister to people on His behalf. Jewish physical symbols, such as mezuzas and phylacteries, are thought of as religious receptacles for spiritual awareness. The feasts

given in the Bible are specific days that, when observed properly, open a "window" of opportunity for the Almighty to
make something good happen for us. When Jewish people
perform mitzvahs, according to Kabbalistic thought, they
align themselves in a positive position in the universe.

The Kabbalistic view of the Messiah is twofold. First, the
Anointed One is a person who teaches the world about spiritual paths to God. The first person with that capability was
believed to be Adam, but he failed. In spite of his failure, he
passed on this "messianic potential" to future generations.
Kabbalists believe that the Messiah can be brought to earth by
righteous living and a proper path to God. If He does not come
within a 6,000-year span (we are nearing the end of that time
period), then His coming will be with destruction and devasta-
tion. The Messiah, it is believed, will be the Son of Man, not
the Son of God.

One of the many notable works in Kabbalah is *Zohar*, the
book of splendor. Written in a secret language, it is a commentary on the Bible. Mastering this text supposedly helps a
person to be in the center of God's will. Another is *Sefer
Yetzira*, the *book of creation*, which tells the creation story
using a complex numbering system.

My Gentile roommate's reason for studying Kabbalah
was interesting, revealing, and even frightening. Involved in
the use of Ouija boards and Tarot cards, he was constantly
searching for higher planes of consciousness. Just as for the
Jewish person who is not satisfied with the plain truth of the
Scriptures, a search for deeper meaning and a higher plane is
very attractive.

Bible-believing Christians understand that there is a
supernatural side to the Bible, with numerous examples of
miracles, angels, spirits, etc. The difference, however,

involves a realization that these things come from God. Humans are in no way able to propel themselves into a higher spiritual plane. Moreover, Scripture warns of the dangers of dealing with any supernatural power other than that which comes from our Lord Himself. May we marvel in the awesome power of God and God alone.

JEWISH FOOD

A SPECIAL DIET

Food, glorious food! We need it to survive! We eat it to celebrate almost any occasion. We offer it in hospitality or comfort. Socially, food somehow helps to build bridges for easier and better communication between people, whether they be friends or strangers. For some, food is in short supply, while others enjoy a wonderful abundance of it.

Special diets or specific preferences for food characterize various cultures. The Jewish people are one such group. Their special food was prescribed by God, presented to His people, and is particular in its preparation.

Having chosen, redeemed, and separated a people for His own, God prescribed a unique lifestyle for them. As a part of that separate lifestyle—which included a dress code, business code, and behavior code—was a dietary code. He presented this diet through His servant Moses, who recorded it in two sections of the Torah: Leviticus 11 and Deuteronomy 14. Contrary to popular belief, this special diet was not given to the Jewish people to promote better health, although it does accomplish that. The dietary code was to set Israel apart from the other nations, to make them a holy people (Leviticus 11:45).

Rules concerning the eating of animals, birds, fish, and insects form the major portion of the code. A *kosher* (*fit* or *proper*) animal must meet two requirements: It must chew its cud and have completely split hooves forming two toes. Kosher fish are required to have fins and scales. Certain fowl—such as ostrich, raven, stork, owl, pelican, and eagle—are not fit for consumption. Three kinds of insects—locusts, crickets, and grasshoppers—are permitted to be eaten, although few people, if any, indulge. None of these creatures can be eaten unless slaughtered specifically for consumption.

While their diet was part of a plan to make the Jewish people peculiar, the great sages and rabbis became even more particular. Exodus 23:19 and Deuteronomy 14:21 prohibit the Jewish people from eating a kid (goat) boiled in its mother's milk, a common practice for the pagans of that day. As a separate people, the Jews were not to participate in such practices. An incredible amount of legislation has been generated from these two verses. This legislation, called *Kashrut* (*proper dietary law*), means that meat dishes and dairy dishes (Yiddish, *fleishig* and *milchig* respectively) cannot be mixed. As a result, a kitchen must have one set of pots, pans, utensils, and dishes to be used in the preparation and consumption of meat dishes and another set for dairy foods. A kosher kitchen is equipped with a double sink, one side for washing milchig dishes, the other side for the fleishig.

The method of killing animals for food has always been addressed by the great sages and rabbis. A *shoket* (*ritual slaughterer*) must do the killing, thus eliminating conventional hunting for observant Jews. A shoket draws a *chalif* (specific *knife*) across the throat of the animal. With one swift cut, the trachea and esophagus are severed. This procedure is regarded as the most humane for the animal and is the best way to drain the blood. The Bible does not allow consumption of fat or blood (Leviticus 3:17). Accordingly, kosher meat must be salted for at least 30 minutes to drain any remaining blood. If this is not done, the rabbis deem the meat to be *traif* (*unclean*).

To assure observant consumers that the food they are purchasing is kosher, agencies certified by the rabbis are used. The most common symbols for kosher are the U and K. P is the symbol for *pareve*, which means *neutral.* Foods considered pareve can be eaten with either meat or dairy and include fruits, vegetables, cereals, coffee—anything grown naturally. Non-dairy milk products can also be considered pareve.

It should be noted that only a small percentage of Jewish people observe the dietary laws, and they do so in varying degrees. Some are very strict and would not so much as drink a glass of water in a non-kosher home. Others keep kosher only in their own homes, while freely dining on non-kosher foods outside the home. For many years it has been an individual choice.

In a day of calorie counting and fat consciousness, people are discovering that the Lord's special diet is very healthful. This should not be surprising. Paul stated that the law is "holy, and just, and good" (Romans 7:12). Equally true is Luke's statement, "What God hath cleansed, that call not thou unclean" (Acts 11:9). Followers of Christ are free to eat (or not eat) whatever they want, providing they know the food was not sacrificed to idols. Sanctification is not accomplished by diet, but by God, as people surrender their lives to Him through Christ. It progresses as we walk in Him. The dietary laws might afford good health, but they will never enhance the spiritual walk of believers. Christ fulfilled the law, and for that we say, "Amen!"

FUSSY FRESSERS

Food is an integral part of Jewish life. One man explained it this way: "For our people, food is more than a necessity of life; it is an emotional experience." *Fressen* is a Yiddish/German word that describes a way of eating. To *fress* is to eat *in a hurry* or to eat *noisily*. A *fresser* is a person who eats in such a manner. For that reason, the word appears on menus in many Jewish restaurants and delis to convey the idea of the relish with which their food is to be enjoyed.

There is a threefold reason for the importance and significance attached to food in the Jewish culture. First, God was very specific in His revelation concerning what is kosher to eat. Second, certain foods are used to celebrate special feast days and other historic Jewish events. Third, a warning of judgment appears in the Talmud for those who fail to enjoy the good things made available to them.

So what is "Jewish" food? If you walked the streets of New York, Los Angeles, Chicago, or even Tel Aviv or Jerusalem, you would see Jews eating everything from pizza to Chinese food (kosher, of course) and enjoying it. A diverse diet has been part of the Jewish experience since the *diaspora* (*dispersion*) in 70 A.D. Using the rules of Kashrut, combined with the cuisine of the country of residence or origin, the Jewish diet is not only unique but varied. Jewish cookbooks abound, featuring recipes that are as easy to prepare as they are mouthwatering.

The best way to get acquainted with Jewish cuisine is to visit a Jewish restaurant or delicatessen. It is a wonderful experience, worth every effort made to accomplish it. So come with me, if you will, to Bernie's, or Lou's, or Al's. The decor is strictly out of the 50s—not nostalgically, but genuinely so. A huge deli counter stocked with savory foods stands to one side. Customers wanting take-out food bark out their orders. The rest of the room is occupied by people seated in booths, conversing enthusiastically with each other. It is the kind of place where you can sit, watch, listen, and be thoroughly entertained.

As you peruse the menu, a puzzled look comes over your face. You must have some of the items translated. If it does not happen forthrightly, you will be forced to do what one gentlemen did when he saw the menu. So overwhelmed at the offerings, he ordered the only item familiar to him, a toasted cheese sandwich. But don't fret, stay calm. Those strange words do represent real food—wonderful, delicious food. So try it. You'll like it!

Under the heading *Brunch* you will see the word *lox.* Taken from the German *lacks* and the Scandinavian *lax,* lox is smoked salmon. It is either *regular* (*salty*) or *nova* (*less salty*). I call it "Jewish gold" because of its high price and wonderful taste. Lox is eaten most commonly on a bagel with cream cheese, onion, and tomato slices. Served with scrambled eggs and onions, it is out of this world.

Also on the brunch menu are salami and eggs; *matzo brei* (*eggs* combined with *unleavened bread*); and *knish* (pronounced ken-ISH), a pocket of dough filled with your choice of potatoes, cheese, onions, pineapples, or just about anything else you might want.

Looking at the lunch menu we see some sumptuous items: chicken soup (sometimes called "Jewish penicillin") with your choice of *matzo balls* (dumplings made of unleavened meal, water, and eggs) or *kreplach* (a pastry pocket stuffed with meat). Or how about a sandwich made with pastrami, corned beef, chopped liver, or tongue? Breads for sandwiches are diverse—bagels, kaiser (hard) rolls, bialy, pumpernickel, or rye, to name a few. Every sandwich comes with a pickle, but not just any pickle. It's a *kosher dill pickle*, the best of all pickles, especially if it has been cured in a wooden pickle barrel.

To wash down that lunch you must have a chocolate phosphate (seltzer mixed with chocolate sauce). On the east coast, milk is added to create a chocolate cream. At many delicatessens, Foxes U-BET™ is the chocolate sauce of choice for phosphates.

Dinner foods are varied and delicious. Chicken is ever-popular, whether roasted, boiled, broiled, or stuffed. Various beef dishes are offered, such as *flanken* (short ribs), stuffed veal breast, stuffed peppers, and brisket. Leg of lamb, breast of lamb, and lamb kabobs are also common.

Side dishes that complement these entrées are varied and tempting. *Kasha* (buckwheat) *varnishkas* (bow-tie noodles), *farfel* (toasted pasta dough), and *kugel* (noodle pudding) are just a few.

And who doesn't like dessert? Honey and coffee cakes are the best, but you should also try the *mandelbrot* (almond bread cookies). The cookies are best when they are rock hard, dipped in a steaming cup of coffee. *Rugalach* are delectable pastries filled with raisins, prunes, poppy seeds, almonds, or any number of sweet fillings.

So, what's your pleasure? Whether you just want to *nosh* (snack) or go ahead and fress, try one of these delicious Jewish delicacies. You'll have a new appreciation of our culture.

FOOD FOR THOUGHT

Food, with its various tastes, smells, textures, and visual appeal, is a powerful trigger in the process of remembering. Whether it is in the preparation, serving, or eating, certain foods seem to prompt many people to close their eyes, take a deep breath, and remember where and when they last indulged.

Since the days of the Bible, the Jewish people have used food to celebrate and remember certain holy days. Because each of these days points to a highlight in Jewish history, a properly prepared menu can ensure not only a tasty and satisfying meal but also a marvelous lesson in Jewish theology.

Sabbath

It has been said, "More than Israel has kept the Sabbath, the Sabbath has kept Israel." Foods served on this day remind the Jewish people of its importance for rest and worship.

Two loaves of yellow braided bread form the centerpiece of countless Sabbath tables. Known as *challahs*, these loaves bring to the Jewish mind the memory of the heavenly bread (manna) that God provided for His people as they wandered in the wilderness for 40 years. Two loaves are used to remember the double portion of manna given for the Sabbath (Exodus 16:22-26). Despite the trauma of their bondage in Egypt, God's Chosen People fondly remembered the fish they ate there (Numbers 11:5). Thus, it is not surprising that eating fish is customary in the Jewish community. Similar to a fish hamburger, *gefilte fish* is made of several different kinds of inexpensive fish. Carp, pike, or whitefish are filleted, combined, and shaped into a patty, then boiled and cooled.

Although it is not eaten much today, *cholent* is a stew made of garlic, onion, beef, beans, eggs, and carrots. Because it cooks for a long time over a low heat, it can be prepared before the Sabbath begins, at which time work, such as lighting a fire, is not permitted.

Passover

The task of planning and preparing a tasty meal without leaven is not easy, yet the Passover feast is eagerly anticipated in most Jewish families. Almost every food item tells a story or serves as a reminder of God's power in delivering His people. At the center of this celebration is *matzo (unleavened bread)*. Matzo ball soup, matzo pancakes, matzo biscuits, and matzo *brei (fried)* are but a few of the imaginative and tasty ways matzo is used.

Haroset, a relish made with apples, nuts, and cinnamon, represents the mortar made by Jewish slaves in Egypt and is a delicious way to remember the sweetness of freedom. And, while eating horseradish may raise the voice an octave, it also serves as a reminder of the bitterness of their bondage.

The absence of lamb is significant. It is purposely omitted from most Jewish Passover tables to lament the sober truth that the Temple is gone, destroyed in 70 A.D.

Shavout

Pentecost (the Feast of Weeks) occurs seven weeks and one day after Passover. It is believed that Moses brought the Ten Commandments down from Mount Sinai on that day. Song of Solomon 4:11 states that "honey and milk are under thy tongue," implying that as dairy foods are pleasant to the taste, so the words of God are pleasant to the soul. Cheese blintzes and strudel are wonderful reminders of this fact.

Purim

"O, once there was wicked, wicked man, and Haman was his name, sir...." This line from a children's song suggests the origin of Purim's best-known food, *Hamantaschen*. These fruit-filled pastries are shaped in triangles because legend says that the villain Haman wore a three-cornered hat. (The actual meaning of *Hamantaschen* is *Haman's pockets.)*

Purim commemorates God's deliverance of the Jews from the evil Haman's plot.

Hanukkah

The miracle of the oil is the theme of this winter holiday. Anything cooked in oil can be used as a reminder. Doughnuts and *latkes* (*potato pancakes*) are two of the favorite dishes of Hanukkah. Dairy products are also popular because of the legend of Judith, the Maccabee daughter who fed the enemy general curds of cheese until he fell asleep and was thus defeated in his sleep. Sour cream and blintzes also are served for this holiday. *Gelt* (*money*) is often given at this time, and so edible, foil-covered coins are also eaten.

It should be pointed out that the most important memories of these celebrations are not necessarily linked to the specific food items. The food serves to symbolize and remind. The most important aspects of each holiday are the people who participate and, above all, the God who commanded us to remember that He must take center stage. As families and friends gather to celebrate, the fellowship around the table makes impressions that last a lifetime.

JEWISH HOLIDAYS

PASSOVER

Praised be Thou, O Lord our God, King of the Universe, who has sanctified us with Thy commandments, and enjoined upon us the mitzvah of kindling the Festival lights....

And, in so saying, Jewish women for centuries have ushered in the festival of Pesach, or Passover, on the 15th day of the month of Nisan. The candles are lit, the prayer is said, and Jewish people the world over begin the ceremony commanded by God Himself: "And thou shalt show thy son in that day, saying, This is done because of that which the LORD did unto me when I came forth out of Egypt" (Ex. 13:8).

The Purpose

Remembering important events has been part of humanity for a long time. God gave the Jewish people many special days for remembering the great things He has done for them. One of the most important of these days is a feast called Passover. Passover reminds the Jewish people of the last meal eaten while they were in bondage in Egypt. It reminds them of their journey—the exodus—from Egypt to the land that God promised. Passover is a reminder of the redemption wrought when the angel of death *passed over* the homes where the blood of a lamb had been applied to the lintels of the doors. The Talmud tells the Jewish people that Passover is to remind adults to "impress, inspire, and educate" the children. It is a happy time, a joyous time, a time to celebrate.

Preparation for the Passover

Jewish people have been spring cleaning for 3,500 years, in obedience to the command found in Exodus 13:7, "no leavened bread [shall] be seen with thee, neither shall there be leaven seen with thee in all thy quarters." The house is cleaned of all leaven before the arrival of the Passover.

Personally, I remember my mother lining the stove, the bread box, and the refrigerator with foil, even after a good cleaning, in the event any leaven had been overlooked. The ancient sages say that leaven symbolizes evil and must be dealt with. To further ensure the absence of even a trace of leaven, special dishes are used, as well as special pots and pans to prepare food, none of which will have any leaven in them.

Participants and Practice

Passover is about families. Exodus 12:1-14 tells us the story. Each person in the family has a role to play. The Passover meal is called the *Seder*, a Hebrew word meaning *order*. The order has been consistent for at least two thousand years.

The *Haggadah* (a book of songs, prayers, and various readings) tells the participants what to do and when to do it. The head of the family (traditionally the father or grandfather) sits at the head of the table and directs the proceedings.

The Seder begins with the woman of the home lighting the Passover candles, in the hope that the light of the candles will light the spirits of the family, followed by the other elements of the Seder.

The *Kiddish* (the *blessing of the wine*): This cup represents the first of the four *I wills* spoken by God in Exodus 6:6-7. "*I will* bring you out from under the burdens of the Egyptians" (v. 6). The wine must be red, to remind the participants of the blood of the lamb.

U-r'hatz (*washing the hands*): Washing is, and always has been, a very important personal and religious function for the Jewish people. Not only does it purify, it also reminds us of the priests as they prepared themselves for service.

Karpas (the *green vegetables*): The participants then take parsley (or any green vegetable) and dip it in a bowl of salt-water. These two elements speak, respectively, of springtime, which is nature's renewal, and of the tears that were shed during the four hundred years of bondage in Egypt. The parsley is also symbolic of the hyssop used to apply the blood to the doorposts.

Yachatz (*breaking the middle matzo*): A pouch containing

three matzos is taken by the leader. The three matzos represent the classifications of Jewish people: the *Kohen*, the *Levites*, and *Israel*. The rabbis say that the three loaves together represent strength in unity. The middle matzo is taken and broken by the leader, wrapped in white, and hidden away. The part that is hidden is called the *Afikomen*, or the *bread of affliction*. It is known in the Passover as the dessert.

The Four Questions: The youngest member of the family has the important task of asking the leader about the Passover and Seder. He wants to know why this night is different from all other nights. He asks:

> On all other nights we eat leaven—why on this night only unleavened bread? On all other nights we eat all kinds of herbs—why on this night only bitter herbs? On all other nights we don't dip even once—why on this night do we dip twice? On all other nights we eat sitting or reclining—why on this night do we eat reclining?

The leader answers these questions by telling the story of the Jewish people to the time when Moses received the Law at Mount Sinai. At this point the second cup of wine is poured. Each participant at the Seder table dips his little finger into his wine and recites, one by one, the ten plagues as he puts the drop of wine onto his own plate. In so doing, the Jewish people remember the suffering even of their enemies. A prayer for the wine is recited and the second cup is taken. This is the second *I will*—"*I will* rid you out of their bondage" (Exodus 6:6).

Pesah (the *Paschal lamb*): There is no lamb in the Passover service today. Instead, the shank bone of a lamb serves as a reminder of the lambs that were sacrificed yearly before the Temple was destroyed two thousand years ago.

Hazeret (the *bitter herbs*) and *Haroset* (a *sweet mixture of apples, nuts, and cinnamon*): These are eaten together, after the hands have been washed a second time. The bitterness of the herbs recalls the bitter bondage of the Jewish people. The sweetness of the Haroset reminds them of the sweetness of freedom—a bittersweet remembrance. It is then customary to eat the *Hillel sandwich*, named after the great sage, Hillel. Horseradish (the bitter herbs) is put between two pieces of matzo. In Hillel's day, a piece of lamb was also used, for Hillel taught that the three biblical elements—bitter herbs, matzo, and the lamb—should all be remembered.

Now, at last, dinner is served, and what a wonderful meal it is! Prior to the destruction of the Temple (70 A.D.), lamb would have been served. Today, however, the traditional meal includes gefilte fish, chicken or roast beef, and kugel. Many desserts unique to Passover are served (such as cakes, brownies, or pastries baked with potato flour, thus unleavened).

After the festive meal, a search is made for the Afikomen. The children search high and low for it, knowing that the one who finds it will receive a reward. The rabbis say that the Afikomen is important because the Seder cannot end until each participant has eaten a small piece of it. In so doing, they are remembering the lamb. Some rabbis believe that, symbolically, the Afikomen is more important than the shank bone.

The third cup is then taken, accompanied by the third *I will*—"*I will* redeem you with an outstretched arm" (Exodus 6:6). Following this third cup of wine, Elijah the prophet is invited to come to the Seder. A place has been reserved for him at the table, with a glass full of wine.

The fourth cup of wine is then taken. It is the last of the four *I wills*—"*I will* take you to me for a people, and I will be to you a God" (Exodus 6:7).

In closing, the Hallel Psalms (113-118) are sung, a prayer is recited, and, in unison, all participants say a hearty, "Next year in Jerusalem!"

Practical Application of the Passover ———

The Feast of Passover was celebrated by Jesus of Nazareth. It was at the Passover that Jesus instituted the Lord's Supper, or communion. The rich symbolism of the Seder service paints a very clear and revealing picture of Jesus as the promised Messiah and Savior, helping us to better understand this ordinance.

Before the Passover begins, there is a thorough search for leaven. The leaven is then removed from the house. In Judaism, leaven symbolizes evil. When a Christian remembers the Lord in communion, he should search his heart to find any sin and get rid of it by confessing it to God (1 Corinthians 11:27-28).

The woman brings the light to the Passover table. Without her, the story of the physical redemption of the Jewish people could not be told. Two thousand years ago, a Jewess named Miriam (we know her as Mary) was the choice vessel of God to bring spiritual redemption to the world. Without her, the story of salvation could not be told.

The three original elements of the Passover were bitter herbs, unleavened bread, and the lamb. Bitter herbs speak of bitter bondage. Believers are to reflect at communion and realize the bitter bondage of sin and the cure for that bondage—the Lamb, Jesus Christ. He was pure, sinless, without spot—just like that unleavened bread.

A great drama takes place with the Afikomen. Three matzos are placed in one pouch. The middle one is taken, broken, wrapped in white, hidden away, found, redeemed, and shared by all. This middle matzo has taken the place of the lamb in importance, as shown by the fact that everyone at the table must partake of it. Traditions associated with the Afikomen add to its drama. European Jews (Ashkenazi) believe it has power to heal the sick. Oriental Jews believe it can calm a stormy sea.

When Christians remember Jesus at communion, they remember that He—the second person in the Godhead—was taken, broken (or killed), hidden away in a tomb, and then raised from the dead. Believers remember Him by taking a little piece of unleavened bread and eating it. The word *Afikomen* is the only Greek word in the Seder. It means *He came*. The Afikomen looks back, not at the Passover lamb bringing physical salvation in Egypt, but at the Savior, the Passover Lamb who brought spiritual salvation to the world. Isaiah described this event when he said, "he was wounded for our transgressions, he was bruised for our iniquities; the chastisement for our peace was upon him, and with his stripes we are healed" (Isaiah 53:5). Isaiah also said, "he is brought as a lamb to the slaughter" (Isaiah 53:7). John the Baptist called Him "the Lamb of God, who taketh away the sin of the world" (John 1:29).

The Jewish people believe that Elijah will announce the Messiah. Each year they set a place for him at the table, waiting and hoping for the announcement. Two thousand years ago Jesus said of John the Baptist, "this is Elijah" (Matthew 11:14). Malachi 4:5 says that Elijah will be sent before "the great and terrible day of the LORD." Could it be that Elijah will be one of the two witnesses described in Revelation 11, who will appear before the Second Coming of Christ? It is an intriguing question.

In Matthew 26, Jesus instituted communion. He took the unleavened bread, symbolic of His pure and spotless body, and the cup, representing His blood. The cup He took was the third cup, the cup of redemption. He did not drink the fourth cup, saying He would not drink it until He drinks it new with us in His Father's Kingdom.

Matthew 26:30 speaks of a hymn the disciples sang. We know the hymns they sang because they are still sung at Passover. They are the Hallel Psalms (113-118). "The stone which the builders refused is become the head of the corner....it is marvelous in our eyes. This is the day which the LORD hath made; we will rejoice and be glad it" (Psalm118:22-24). *This* is the day. On the first night Jesus celebrated the Passover, and on the second He became the Passover Lamb on behalf of us all. The lamb had to be perfect with no spot or blemish. "He [God the Father] hath made him [Jesus the Son], who knew no sin, to be sin for us" (2 Corinthians 5:21). The lamb was sacrificed. "Christ, our passover, is sacrificed for us" (1 Corinthians 5:7).

The lesson is simple. Jewish or Gentile, old or young, rich or poor—on that night in Egypt, the only issue was whether or not the blood was on the doorpost. Sincerity did not count. Good deeds did not count. Degrees and pedigrees did not count. If the blood of the lamb was on the door, death did not come. If there was no blood, death was a certainty.

The requirements have not changed for us today. God still demands a blood sacrifice to atone for sin. But the amazing news is that God Himself provided that sacrifice in His own Son. The price has been paid.

Jesus said, "I am the way, the truth, and the life; no man cometh unto the Father, but by me" (John 14:6).

Is Christ your Passover Lamb?

SHABBAT

Holidays are commemorative days used by most people to participate in recreational activities, travel, or just relax. Conversely, holy days are special days set aside for worship. Holidays provide a time of release from the everyday pursuit of pleasure. Holy days provide a time to release ourselves to please God through song, prayer, and meditation. Many people enjoy a holiday, but far fewer experience a holy day. In Exodus 20:8-10, God commanded the Israelites to observe a holy day (*Yom Kadosh*) on a weekly basis.

Judaism considers the *Shabbat* (*Sabbath*) observance to be the high point of the week. It is a day of delight, a jewel, a bride, a queen. So important a day is it that some believe if it were properly observed by all Jewish people, the world to come would be ushered in. Biblically, violation of *Yom Kippur* (the *Day of Atonement*, considered the most holy day in Judaism) resulted in excommunication (Leviticus 23:29), but violation of Shabbat, a day "holy to the LORD" (Exodus 31:15), resulted in death.

For the Jewish people, Shabbat memorializes two incredible and miraculous events. It is regarded as the climax of creation. God worked for six days and rested on the seventh (Genesis 2:2). Mankind, therefore, must emulate God and do the same. *Work* is defined as *any activity that creates, produces, or transforms for use.* The second event memorialized is the Exodus, when God freed His people from the Egyptian taskmasters. Shabbat provides a weekly liberation from the *taskmasters* of life. Concerns about occupations, chores at home, school, and other stresses of life are set aside on this day. Shabbat is a day for Jewish people to revitalize and rejuvenate themselves spiritually, emotionally, and physically.

Although the topic of *family values* is popular in current news, it is nothing new in the observant Jewish community. Families have always been an integral part of the seventh-day observance. On at least this one day each week, family members eat, pray, sing, and read together and generally spend time with one another.

A great deal of preparation goes into the Shabbat observance. Jobs are completed early, the house is prepared, and special dishes are used. About 20 minutes before sundown, the woman of the home lights two candles, one to "Remember the...day" (Ex. 20:8) and one to "Keep the... day" holy (Deuteronomy. 5:12). A benediction is then recited, and a warm greeting of "*Shabbat Shalom!*" (*Sabbath peace*) is proclaimed.

The family then attends the Friday evening service (*Kabbalot Shabbat*) at the synagogue. Upon returning home, the father blesses his children, quoting Numbers 6:24-27, with his hand placed on their heads. Next, the *Kiddush* (prayer over the wine) is recited, and two loaves of *challah* (braided egg bread) are broken. Two loaves are used because in Exodus 16:22 God told the Israelites to gather a double portion of manna the day before Shabbat. Finally, the first of three Shabbat meals is eaten. The menu varies but usually includes gefilte fish, chicken soup, chicken or beef, and wonderful baked desserts.

There is no sleeping in on Saturday morning because the family must be at synagogue early, usually by 8:30 a.m. There prayers are chanted and sung, the Torah scrolls are opened and read, and the rabbi delivers a sermon. The service lasts about three hours and is followed with an *Oneg Shabbat* (*delight in the Sabbath*), a time of *noshing* (*snacking*), and fellowship.

Back at home after the service, the second of the three Shabbat meals is eaten, and a time of leisure follows. Driving, shopping, watching television, and even switching on lights—all considered forms of work—are forbidden. Instead, time is spent reading, walking, visiting, playing board games, and sleeping.

The third meal is eaten in the late afternoon, and the *Maariv* (*evening*) service follows. At this service the *Havdalah* (*division*) is recited over a cup of wine, fragrant spices, and a special double-braided candle called *Havdalah*. This short but symbol-filled service illustrates the beauty, majesty, and holiness of the day. This holy day is anticipated with great joy, and sadness is felt at its departure. About 40 minutes after sundown, the *queen* has left for another week.

Setting a day aside for rest and worship is both biblical and practical. The Old Testament taught the Jewish people to look forward to a day of rest. The New Testament stresses that believers should start off with His rest and then move forward. Of the Ten Commandments, only the fourth, regarding Shabbat, is not mentioned in the New Testament. During this dispensation we are not obligated to keep the law. Yet the principles of Shabbat—commitment to God, celebration with worship, camaraderie that builds up family and friends, and the sense of community fostered among those of like mind—would all serve to strengthen the body of Christ.

THE QUESTION OF TIME

It is often joked about among Jewish people that whenever the time is set for an appointment or a date, the time specified will not be the actual time to begin. It is understood—even as people are arriving late for the wedding, bar mitzvah, or other event—that the clock is ticking on "Jewish time." This somewhat annoying yet insignificant feature in many circles of Jewish life takes on larger proportions in the timing of the various Jewish holidays.

In my family, a conversation took place each year just before the Jewish New Year, Rosh Hashanah. The question always arose, "Are they [the holidays] going to be early or late this year?" Knowing that holidays have fixed dates, how could such a question even be raised? A glance at any Jewish periodical will yield the answer. Two dates can be seen. The date most familiar to us comes from the Gregorian calendar and is used in most countries around the world. The other date is religious, taken from the Jewish calendar. These calendars have numerous differences. The names of the months are different; the number of days in a year is different; their leap years are different; even the number of months in a year is sometimes different.

The Jewish calendar measures a day, not chronologically, but by daylight. Each new day begins after the sun has gone down. The new day begins in the dark and lasts until the following sundown. For example, Tuesday at 10 p.m., according to the Gregorian calendar, is really Wednesday morning, according to the Jewish calendar. This means that summer days are longer than winter days. The Jewish calendar bases the measurement of each month on the appearance of the new moon. A lunar month—the length of time it takes for the moon to make one revolution around the earth—lasts 29 1/2 days. Thus, the 12 Jewish months alternate between 29 and 30 days.

The beginning of each month or new moon is considered a holy day. In Old Testament days, the *shofar*, or *trumpet*, was blown while burnt offerings were given as a memorial before the Lord (Numbers 10:10). The new month or new moon is known as *Rosh Hodesh* (*the head of the month*). Since the destruction of the Temple, the celebration of the new moon has become less significant, but to this day it is observed with special prayers recited on its arrival.

Twelve lunar months of 29 ½ days yield 354 days, a difference of 11 days each year from our solar calendar. The Bible mandates that holidays be kept in their "appointed season" (Numbers 9:2-3). In light of that mandate, periodic adjustments must be made with the calendar. Therefore, one leap *month* is added seven times every 19 years. It is during these times that the Jewish calendar shifts from the customary 12 months to 13 months.

The Jewish calendar bases its year on Judaism's traditional belief that the earth was created 3,761 years before Christ. Thus, to establish the Jewish year, simply add the number of the current Gregorian year to 3,761. To avoid designating Christ as Lord, the Jewish calendar uses B.C.E. (*before the common era*) or C.E. (*common era*) instead of B.C. (*before Christ*) and A.D. (*Anno Domini, in the year of our Lord*).

Until the year 359 A.D., the arrival of the new moon was announced by the Sanhedrin, the supreme judicial body for Jewish life, and was based on the testimony of two eyewitnesses. They had to appear before a special council to answer questions about the sighting of the thin, visible crescent of the new moon. If the council was satisfied with the information given by the two witnesses, they would process it with their own secret astrological and mathematical formulas. If, after all of that, the information proved reliable, the Sanhedrin would send torch signals from mountaintop to mountaintop to notify all of the communities in Israel that the new moon had been officially sighted. In the year 360 A.D., the Sanhedrin's closely guarded formulas for determining the new moon became public information and ultimately led to their declining power. Today, anyone can secure a copy of a Jewish calendar. It provides a wealth of information, including the exact time of the sunset, when to light the Sabbath candles, corresponding Gregorian dates, and other timely facts.

So, what difference does the timing of the Jewish calendar make to us? Much, in every way. First, it ties the Bible reader to the times and seasons in which the biblical feasts—feasts that Jesus celebrated—were observed. Second, questions on the sequence of time involved in the death, burial, and resurrection of Christ can be readily answered. Third, it can explain why anniversary dates in Israel might not be the same as ours. (The anniversary of Israeli Prime Minister Rabin's assassination is November 4 on the Gregorian calendar, but the date on the Jewish calendar is Cheshvan 12, which fell on October 25 the first year after his death, a difference of 10 days.) Finally, it reiterates the great care given to detail in Judaism—even to the question of time.

HEBREW MONTH	HOLIDAY	GREGORIAN MONTHS
Nisan (30 days)	Passover (14th) Unleavened Bread (15th-21st) Holocaust Memorial Day (27th)	March-April
Iyyar (29 days)	Israel Independence Day (5th) 33rd Day of Omer (18th) Jerusalem Day (28th)	April-May
Sivan (30 days)	Pentecost (6th)	May-June

HEBREW MONTH	HOLIDAY	GREGORIAN MONTHS
Tammuz (29 days)		June-July
Av (30 days)	Ninth of Av	July-August
Elul (29 days)		August-September
Tishri (30 days)	New Year (1st) Day of Atonement (10th) Tabernacles (15th-22nd)	September-October
Cheshvan (29 or 30 days, "swing month")		October-November
Kislev (29 or 30 days, "swing month")	Hanukah (15th), for 8 days	November-December
Tevat (30 days)		December-January
Shvat (30 days)	T'u B'Shvat (15th)	January-February
Adar (29 days)	Purim (14th)	February-March

Adar II (one month added 7 times in 19 years (3rd, 6th, 8th, 11th, 14th, 17th, and 19th years)

Mazel Tov
Nosh
Kinder
Kosher
Shiva
Yente
Schmooz
Gonif
Kibbutz
Gevalt
Shlep

A JEWISH VOCABULARY

FERMISHED AND FERBLONJET

A guide is a person who shows the way by leading, directing, or advising. The Friends of Israel uses excellent guides on our tours to Israel. These individuals provide insightful information as they lead us through the Holy Land. From time to time our "flock" of travelers goes astray, quickly becoming overwhelmed by the crowds and confusion. I have noticed a common look on their faces when we manage to locate them— a look of bewilderment. In Yiddish we would say they looked *fermished* and *ferblonjet—bewildered* and *confused.*

I have seen that same look on the faces of people who are hearing Yiddish for the first time. Many Yiddish words and expressions have become familiar to us; others remain obscure. Permit me to be your guide through a selected glossary of Yiddish terms.

Bagel (BA-gel): Doughnut-shaped bread. Originally available only in plain or egg flavors, they now come with onion, garlic, sesame seeds, and other wonderful combinations.

Bashert (Ba-SHERT): A common expression heard from the lips of Jewish people, "What is bashert is bashert" or "What will be will be."

Bobe Myseh (BOO-bee MY-se): A made-up story; an old wives' tale.

Boobe (BOO-bee): An affectionate term, similar to darling or honey.

Boychik (BOY-chick): Literally, a boy, but used with great affection.

Bubbe (BUB-bee): A grandmother.

Chazzer (HA-zer): Literally, a pig; used of someone who is selfish.

Chutzpa (HOOT-spa): Having guts, gall, nerve, or arrogance.

Ferblonjet (Fer-BLON-jet): Confused.

Fermished (Fer-MISHED): Bewildered.

Forshpeis (FOR-shpeese): An appetizer.

Fress/Fresser (FRES-ser): To eat a lot; one who eats a lot.

Gelt: Literally, gold; money.

Get: A divorce.

Gevalt (Ge-VALT): Used with the word *Oy*, it is an expression of astonishment or amazement.

Gonif (GON-if): A thief; sometimes used of an untrustworthy person.

Goy/Goyim (Goy-IM): A Gentile; Gentiles.

Haymish (HAY-mish): An unspoiled, warm, or unpretentious person.

Kibbutz (Kib-BUTZ): Communal living in Israel; not to be confused with...

Kibitz (KIB-bits): To chatter on and on.

Kinder (KIN-der): Children.

Kinehora (Kin-e-HOR-a): A superstitious term used to protect people from evil coming upon them.

Klezmer (KLEZ-mer): Traditional music from Eastern Europe, performed today in various celebrations and coffee shops.

Kosher (KO-sher): Fit or proper; can be used of food, clothes, business.

Kvell (K-VELL): To beam with pride.

Kvetch (K-VETCH): To complain; a complainer.

Macher (MA-cher): The big cheese; the head honcho; the one with all the connections.

Maven (MAV-en): The expert or know-it-all.

Mazel Tov (MAZ-el Tov): An expression of good luck or congratulations.

Megillah (Me-GIL-lah): The whole story.

Mensch: A good person; one who is helpful and kind.

Meshugena (Me-SHOOG-e-na): Crazy, nutty, or wacky.

Mishegas (MISH-e-gas): Craziness, absurdity.

Mishpocha (Mish-PO-ha): Family.

Naches (NA-ches): A delightful feeling of pride that comes when children get married, graduate from school, or receive a promotion.

Nudnick (NOOD-nick): A pest; someone who gets on your nerves.

Nosh: A snack.

Schmooz (SHMOO-ze): Friendly chatter.

Seychel (SAY-chel): Common sense.

Shamaltz: Rendered fat, usually chicken fat.

Shaygets (SHA-gets): A male Gentile.

Shikse (SHIK-sa): A female Gentile.

Shiva (SHIV-a): A seven-day period of mourning when a loved one dies.

Shlemiel (Shl-MEEL): Someone who never seems to get it right.

Shlep: To drag along.

Shlepper (SHLEP-per): Behind; a person who appears discombobulated.

Shlock: Shoddy or cheap junk.

Shmatte (SHMA-ta): A rag; cheap clothing.

Shnorrer (SHNOR-er): A moocher.

Shonda (SHON-da): A scandal.

Shtick: A thing.

Tsuris (TZER-is): Trouble.

Yente (YEN-tee): A gossipy woman.

Yiddishe kop (YID-ish-a CUP): Literally, a Jewish head; clever.

Zayde (ZA-dee): A grandfather.

If you master this short glossary, you will *kvell* with pride. *Kinehora*, what sounded like *mishegas* to you before has transformed you into a *maven*.

EPILOGUE

You have just taken a short guided tour through the vast forest of Jewish culture and customs. By no means exhaustive, this volume is meant to be the reader's introduction to some of the marvelous aspects of Judaism.

Gaining knowledge merely for the sake of knowledge is commendable at best, self-serving at its worst. Using that knowledge to a positive advantage becomes a blessing to everyone involved. It is my desire that any insight you have acquired in reading this book will be used of the Lord to give you a better understanding of your Jewish friends. As you come to know and appreciate these people chosen by God Himself, may He use you to be a testimony to them of His great love.

RECOMMENDED READING

Agus, Jacob Bernard. *The Meaning of Jewish History*. (New York: Abelard-Schuman, 1963.)

Dimont, Max. *Jews, God, and History*. Signet Books. (New York: Simon and Schuster, 1962.)

Finkelstein, Lois, ed. *The Jews*. (New York: Schocken Books, 1972.)

Golden, Hyman. *The Jew and His Duties*. (New York: Hebrew Publishing Company, 1953.)

Grayzel, Solomon. *A History of the Jews*. (Philadelphia, PA: The Jewish Publication Society of America, 1947.)

Johnson, Paul. *History of the Jews*. (New York: Harper and Row, 1987.)

Klapperman, Gilbert and Libby. *The Story of the Jewish People*, vols. 1-4. (New York: Behrman House, Inc., 1956, 1957, 1961.)

Kolatch, Alfred J. *The Jewish Book of Why*, vols. 1-2. (Middle Village, NY: Jonathan David Publishers, 1981, 1985.)

Pessin, Deborah. *The Jewish People*. (New York: United Synagogue Commission on Jewish Education, 1952.)

Telushkin, Rabbi Joseph. *Jewish Literacy*. (New York: William Morrow and Company, 1991.)